GREEN WEDDING

GREEN WEDDING

PLANNING YOUR ECO-FRIENDLY CELEBRATION

Mireya Navarro

STEWART, TABORI & CHANG
NEW YORK

Published in 2009 by Stewart, Tabori & Chang
An imprint of Harry N. Abrams, Inc.

Library of Congress Cataloging-in-Publication Data:

Navarro, Mireya.
  Green wedding : planning your eco-friendly celebration / by Mireya Navarro.
     p. cm.
  Includes index.
  ISBN 978-1-58479-712-8
  1. Weddings—United States—Planning. 2. Weddings—Environmental aspects—United States. 3. Green movement—United States. I. Title.
  HQ745.N37 2009
  395.2'2–dc22   2008029124

Editor: Dervla Kelly
Designer: Pamela Geismar
Production Manager: Tina Cameron

The text of this book was composed in Gotham and Excelsior.

Printed and bound in the United States of America

10 9 8 7 6 5 4 3 2 1

Mixed Sources
Product group from well-managed forests, controlled sources and recycled wood or fiber
www.fsc.org Cert no. BV-COC-080720
© 1996 Forest Stewardship Council
FSC

HNA
harry n. abrams, inc.
a subsidiary of La Martinière Groupe

115 West 18th Street
New York, NY 10011
www.hnabooks.com

PAGE 2 A 40-foot-high glass façade provides a dramatic backdrop for weddings at Barr Mansion, a green formal venue in Austin, Texas.

To my husband, Jim

CONTENTS

When I found my soul mate, I was already in my forties, and I'd had plenty of time to figure out what I didn't like in weddings. I loved seeing my friends jubilant on their big day, and I'd had my share of fun at the parties. But I had also developed a distaste for the formulaic staging of many weddings—I felt they all managed to end up looking more or less the same—and I was appalled by the expense some couples endured. When my turn came, I was clear. "Why don't we elope to Vegas?" I asked my fiancé, Jim. "Sounds good," my once-divorced betrothed replied. "But . . ."

There *were* other things to consider. I thought about my aging, and very traditional mother, who had waited decades to marry me off. My poor dad had long given up on me, but he was thrilled when Jim formally asked him for my hand, shortly before he passed away. I also realized my wedding would be something of a reunion with people who had meant everything to me when I was growing up in Puerto Rico. Schoolmates from my parish school, neighbors who had picked me up after I skinned my knees in the street, my parents' many close friends, relatives scattered all over the island and a few on the mainland. How else would they all meet my Prince Charming? Most of all, I pictured my mom, looking glorious and proud while reveling in the role of mother of the bride.

So we decided to have a real wedding in San Juan in 2005, and it was everything I had hoped for. It was a sentimental journey, and I felt surrounded by love. The wedding was even a bit extravagant, since we held it in a historic hotel, but with careful planning we were able to economize and simplify. For instance, we live in Los Angeles, and we decided we would have a two-part movable feast so that most guests wouldn't have to fly. The civil ceremony and reception were at the Hotel El Convento in Old San Juan with about seventy guests. We followed up with a second set of vows under a Huppah in our backyard with another seventy or so friends and family. In Puerto Rico, we chose the "island" menu the hotel offered, which was cheaper and meant using local fare, such as sweet plantains, pumpkin soup, and paella. For the invitations to our California house party, we

used electronic Evites, avoiding paper waste. Ultimately, my wedding was on the lighter shade of green without really trying. That was before my own environmental consciousness had kicked into higher gear.

Two years later, all that would change. Doing research for an article for the Sunday *New York Times*, I encountered a smart new world of couples who were making conscious decisions to have green weddings. They calculated the mileage their guests would travel to offset wedding-related carbon dioxide emissions. Some brides were recycling by wearing used gowns. Some grooms were wearing recycled gold rings. Food was local and organic. The coffee was Fair Trade. But many of these weddings still adhered to tradition. For these couples, what mattered was a wedding that celebrated their union and their commitment to protecting the environment from wasteful and damaging consumption.

An environmentally sound wedding may sound sanctimonious to some—especially to that relative or friend who will also find fault with your choice of venue or— God forbid!—groom. But many young adults preparing to launch careers and families find the idea of a green wedding appealing because, at any budget, it steers them toward spending their money more wisely. Today, when some couples worry about the wedding from hell, it is not just concern over lost invitations or a missing officiant, or the possibility that Uncle Virgil will get drunk (again), steal the microphone, and serenade the newlyweds with a slurred version of "Feelings." Instead, they fret over spending thousands of dollars on flowers that will wilt away, on a gown that will never be worn again, and on

party gifts that will go straight into the trash. And how about all that fuel-burning travel by out-of-town guests? More and more couples are saying: There's a better way.

"I want our wedding to reflect our values," one bride told me. For her and the many other brides and grooms I interviewed for this book, as well as members of a new generation of wedding planners, those values include a new sense of responsibility: holding ourselves accountable for our contributions to the planet's woes.

More and more Americans want to go beyond empty gestures as the warning signs of global warming become more apparent. "I really believe our world is going quickly downhill, and nothing will be left for our kids," says Kelly Nichols, 26, a production coordinator in a marketing company from Danville, California, who had her green wedding in the fall of 2007. A revolution is afoot, led by the conviction that doing nothing is no longer acceptable.

Think of the staggering spending checklist for a wedding: rings, invitations, registries, flowers, attire, venue, honeymoon, and the catering for dozens, if not hundreds, of guests. What an opportunity to put your values in action. Brides and grooms are reconceiving their weddings to express this new ethical sensibility. Green nuptials, many brides and grooms told me, have less to do with following a trend than reflecting what you care about.

"It doesn't make sense to me that the wedding industry can be so wasteful and gluttonous," says Ali Wood, 32, a creative art therapist from Brooklyn, New York, who got married in May 2008. "You see invitations with ten pieces of paper. For me that isn't representative of who we are and how we live."

Kelly Nichols says of her efforts to go green with most elements of her wedding: "I was proud of the things I did do and guilty about the things I didn't do. But people don't make a change until feeling guilty."

Perhaps guilt is a driving force for some people, but the purpose of this book is not to guilt trip you. The aim is to demonstrate that you can still have the wedding of your dreams while protecting the environment and adding an extra touch of passion to your nuptials. As a detached observer with no stake in either the wedding industry or the environmental lobby, my goal is to tell you why you should consider going green at this wonderful event, discuss the impact your pocketbook decisions can have, describe how to find green products and services, and warn you about the challenges still facing green consumers. Do a Google search for "green weddings" and you will find enough links and vendors—many of them true believers, others just opportunists—to make your head spin. It can be a confusing marketplace; the field is still relatively young. At times I've been tied up in knots separating fact from fiction, trying to extract the one nugget of advice I could give you. Did you hear the one about avoiding the tossing of rice because rice is bad for birds? "Baloney," says Greg Butcher, director of conservation for the National Audubon Society. "Birds eat rice all the time. It wouldn't hurt them."

This book will help you sort through the myths, contradictions, dilemmas, and the offerings in the ever-expanding green wedding sub-industry with an informed eye. It is a book about ideas more than a list of resources, although you'll find plenty of suggestions to get your search started.

You'll learn how to maneuver through marketing claims and resistant guests to reach your green goals. Yes, some of your loved ones may roll their eyes at the registry directing them to donate to the World Wildlife Fund rather than to purchase a new set of towels. They may still get you the electric knife. But you'll see how green weddings are upending traditional wedding etiquette and inspiring friends and relatives to follow you along a greener path. You'll learn new concepts and ideas useful for any celebration, not just a wedding or commitment ceremony, and for living a greener lifestyle. More importantly, you'll hear from pioneering brides and grooms who already planned a green wedding and shared their experiences and lessons.

Some of you are already ahead of the curve in environmental awareness, while some of you may just be starting to learn what carbon offsets are all about. You'll find *Green Wedding* useful either way.

For some couples the goal is to go all green, from ring to honeymoon. For many others, the goal may be to incorporate green elements that best suit their tastes and needs. Most of the brides I interviewed greened some elements, such as the invitations or the food, and not others. Some environmental purists will tell you that the best green wedding is the one that doesn't happen at all. Anything else would be tinkering around the edges. Elope, they say. On a bicycle. If that sounds like a good idea to you, by all means embrace the simplicity.

Kristi Papenfuss and Joshua Houdek found their romantic green venue in Gale Woods Farm, set in a 410-acre park in Minnetrista, Minnesota.

But major environmental organizations support green weddings for their potential to spread the green message effectively and to help steer the multi billion-dollar wedding industry toward greener practices. And in the colossal fight against climate change, every effort counts. If you want a more traditional approach—if, like me, you want to involve your family and loved ones in this major life event—this book will show you how to do it and still do well by the environment.

Bridezillas—brides who are transformed into tyrannical monsters of consumption—are belittled for good reason, but in my view not going all-green does not put a bride in that category. If you picked up this book, or someone who loves you has bought it for you, you likely already care enough to want to do more. So take what suits you. This is your wedding, your moment, and these are your memories. Follow your heart.

I hope *Green Wedding* helps you successfully carry out your ambitious nuptials—ambitious not as an expression of wealth, but of who you really are.

CHAPTER 1

WHAT IS A GREEN WEDDING?

Meet global warming, the villain of our times. While scientists have long been discussing the problem, it broke through our collective consciousness in the first decade of the twenty-first century, most dramatically in 2007, the year of *An Inconvenient Truth*, "Live Earth" concerts, Al Gore's Nobel Peace Prize, and the sudden proliferation of words like *green*, *eco*, and *carbon footprint* in popular culture. It meant the earth was running a temperature—accompanied by melting ice caps, rising seas, and a range of potentially calamitous problems for crops, animals, and ecosystems—and it was all our fault.

We burned fossil fuels at an extraordinary rate, pouring billions of tons of carbon dioxide into the

atmosphere, while we rapidly destroyed the forests that naturally absorb those greenhouse gases. We drove cars, flew in fuel-chugging jetliners, ate meat, and ran clothes dryers at will. Only a minority of us gave much thought to how our habits threw ever more greenhouse gases into the air, trapping the sun's heat near the planet's surface. Who was the world's largest emitter of carbon dioxide, the main heat-trapping gas produced by human activity? The United States, until China took the lead in the mid 2000s. Lifestyle changes were called for to reduce our carbon footprint—our personal contribution to the atmospheric mess.

There's no practical way to be truly carbon-neutral. But we can, and many of us have begun, to take significant steps to mitigate the threat to the planet by switching to fuel-efficient cars and buying more energy-efficient appliances. Some of us are going deeper by changing our diets, turning to renewable energy sources, transforming our homes, and joining groups to pressure the government into action.

Why bother? You only need to read the news. As I write this, I just heard about the Global Seed Vault in Norway, a cave-like structure in the middle of a frozen Arctic mountain built to store samples of the world's seeds as climate change renders some plant species extinct. The polar bear is threatened by vanishing sea ice. The polar bear! A United Nations panel has spelled it out for us. It predicts a slow march toward a global disaster—droughts, food and water shortages, disruptions of habitats—if governments around the world don't work to curb greenhouse gas emissions immediately.

A GREEN WEDDING PRIMER

In light of this mammoth challenge, what can a wedding do? This is an occasion for joy, to express love, to cut loose. Would it really make a difference if couples served locally grown food or if the bride walked down the aisle in a used gown bought on Craigslist? The answer is an absolute yes. The United States produces twice or more the amount of carbon dioxide emissions per person than most countries. Anything each of us can do to shrink this country's size 11 carbon footprint, compared to most of the world's size 5, would help. You want the best memories of this wonderful day, of course, but your wedding can be more than a one-time fantasy. It's an occasion to put on display your values and your commitment to a lifestyle that says the future can be brighter if we take personal responsibility for change. In supporting green products and services, in setting an example for guests who may not have a clue what *sustainable* means, in reflecting your environmental concerns, the green wedding makes a statement that will resonate long after your vows.

"This is a huge industry, and every choice for a green wedding builds the momentum for an entire industry to shift practices," says Audrey Peller, a manager with Global Footprint Network (www.FootprintNetwork.com), an international nonprofit organization with offices in Oakland, California, that promotes sustainability. "Every little bit you do counts," she says. "This is a great way to share your beliefs with the community and inspire others to make eco-friendly choices."

A green wedding is wise in its choices while still tailored to suit your dreams. The goal is to minimize the event's carbon footprint, which is largely the product of the number of guests and how far they are traveling for the celebration. But you can rethink every aspect of the big event. You can question tradition and do without some elements. But whether the wedding is in your backyard or at an elegant hotel, some general guidelines apply:

A reusable grocery bag holds flip-flops and other unwrapped gifts for the bridal party.

◎ the number of guests who have to fly or drive long distances should be minimal.

◎ the invitations shouldn't require destroying trees.

◎ the bride's dress should have a second or third life.

◎ the registry should not be just about "us."

◎ the flowers should not be grown or cut by exploited workers.

◎ the food should be local, seasonal, and not grown with dangerous pesticides (and it should have never said "moo").

◎ any party favors should be more useful than a plastic trinket.

Sometimes religious and cultural imperatives dictate what to wear and what to eat. Being green is not an absolute; it is a series of goals, and only you can decide how far you will go in achieving them. The shade of green in your green wedding may also depend on the budget and what's available near your venue. But whether all green, light green, or, as one bride put it, "relatively green," a green wedding stands against waste and excess. Ask yourself: How can we use less? Do we really need it?

To ward off overconsumption, follow the three "R's"— reduce, reuse, and recycle. "This whole movement," says Delilah Snell, owner of The Road Less Traveled, a green store in Southern California, "is about 'Stop and think— is there an alternative?'"

Green principles will give you a much-needed reality check as you grapple with the emotions and stresses of wedding planning. If you risk drowning in the 100-item to-do checklist, a green wedding throws you a no-waste life ring. It gives you the armor to fend off unwanted pressures from relatives, friends, or vendors trying to convince you to spend lavishly on fancy tablecloths or flower arrangements. It adds clarity and sorts out priorities and choices. "That's not green!" you can respond to a pushy helper, and move on.

But rest assured that your wedding can be green and still distinctly your own. No one need know that the colorful shawls wrapped over the backs of the chairs to keep guests warm were made of recycled plastic bottles— unless you want them to.

"You don't have to compromise the aesthetic of the event," says Danielle Venokur, owner of dvGreen (www.dvgreen.com), a high-end sustainable events production company in New York City. "You just have to find the right vendors."

HOW TO TELL THE GREEN VENDOR FROM THE GREEN WASHER

Here's how to tell the real green vendor from the green washer—the one jumping on the green bandwagon without doing much for the environment.

1. Look for trustworthy labels. Many products are certified by outside parties to vouch for their green credentials. USDA Organic, from the United States Department of Agriculture, means that anything with that label is free of most conventional pesticides. "Fair Trade Certified," for chocolate, honey, and other products means a premium has been paid to producers so they can invest in their communities. Other reliable labels: LEED, for construction and buildings, and Energy Star, for electric appliances.

Under the USDA National Organic Program, a product can be labeled "made with organic ingredients" as long as at least 70 percent of its ingredients are indeed certified organic. Learn which non-organic ingredients you don't want and which ones you can live with—then decide what to buy.

2. Do research when there's no seal of approval. You can:

◎ Go to the vendor's website to look at its environmental policy and record of commitment to sustainable practices. The transparent ones vouch for their products in detail.

◎ Check with watchdogs. Consumer groups like Consumer's Union (whose guide to environmental products and services is found at www.GreenerChoices. org) and The Campaign for Safe Cosmetics (www.SafeCosmetics. org) keep an eye on the green market. Another website, www. GreenwashingIndex.com, offers consumer ratings of environmental claims in ads. The Federal Trade Commission (www.ftc. gov) has guidelines on how to flag misleading environmental advertising.

◎ Look at green guides, such as Co-op America's "National Green Pages" (www.CoopAmerica.org), a directory of businesses screened for environmental practices.

3. Ask questions. A deer-caught-in-the-headlights look or a long pause on the other end of the telephone may be all you need to tell who's who. You may ask of vendors: What are your environmental practices? About products: Where does this come from? How far is it shipped? Of venues: What do you do with the garbage? Do you recycle? Of ecotourism hotels and tour operators: How many of your workers are natives? What are you doing for the local community? Of caterers: Who are your local farmers?

FINDING THE RIGHT VENDORS

Think about it. More than two million marriages take place in the United States each year. For many of us, the wedding budget represents one of the biggest chunks of money we will ever spend in one go. Even couples who rebel against bridal magazines' to-do lists end up spending more than they may have anticipated. A wedding is the biggest party most of us will ever throw.

In looking to spend your money wisely, it is sometimes difficult to distinguish the real green vendors from the

White tablecloths and throw blankets tied with orange ribbons lend a touch of elegance to a reception in the woods.

"green washers," those whose products or services don't live up to their promises (see "How To Tell The Green Vendor From The Green Washer" on page 20.) By the same token, some legitimate vendors don't always advertise themselves as green. Kelly Nichols says she found the green venue for her October 2007 wedding—Wildwood Acres Resort in Lafayette, California—only after she narrowed her search to "state-owned" and "family-owned" properties. "Then I asked the right questions: Do you recycle? Do you use pesticides on your plants?" Kelly says.

You want to support vendors you can relate to, who are not oblivious to environmental warnings, and who have made serious efforts to change their ways. If you know what to look for, it isn't that hard to spot who's walking the walk.

Christine Saunders (TheSpiraledStem.com), a flower designer in Anaheim, California, uses mostly Veriflora-certified flowers (see Chapter 6: The Décor for more about flowers) and has a cash rebate program for couples who return the flower containers after the wedding, to make sure they are not thrown away. Gerald Prolman, founder and CEO of Organic Style Limited and a pioneer of the sustainable flower market in 2001 when he launched OrganicBouquet.com, compensates for the greenhouse gas emissions from his companies' shipping with carbon offsets (for more on offsetting carbon emissions, see Chapter 7: The Guests). Many vendors also donate a percentage of their profits to conservation efforts.

You'll also find wedding and event planners who specialize in green celebrations. Ask about their journeys to green careers—and the criteria they use to vet the vendors—to judge whether their commitment matches yours. Don't be afraid to ask for green practices in vendor contracts. Be wary of "recommendations" from green wedding websites that are thinly disguised vehicles for advertisers. And if you don't find the green product you want, stomp your feet and demand it.

"Retailers don't want to miss the market," notes Prolman. "Take a stand for the environment. When you go to the store and you don't see it, you should ask the retailer, 'Why don't I see it?' Leave a message in the suggestion box. The retailers will listen and respond if they hear that enough people are asking."

Products these days are sold not just on the basis of size or price but also on the strength of labels like "sustainable," "Fair Trade," "local," and "organic" (see "Say What" on page 176). But accurate labeling is a work in progress, and sometimes it can feel as anarchic as the Wild West.

Take the "natural" products industry. It got a kick in the pants in March 2008 when the watchdog group Organic Consumers Association (www.OrganicConsumers.org) announced that tests on "natural" or "organic" shampoos, body washes, and other personal care and household cleaning products showed the presence of the cancer-causing chemical 1,4-dioxane, a byproduct of the petrochemicals used in their manufacturing process. It was a stark reminder that the "natural" and "organic" veneer is sometimes just that. The consumers group advises "buyer beware" unless the product is certified under the United States Department

of Agriculture National Organic Program and carries the USDA Organic label.

This doesn't necessarily mean all uncertified companies are bad, or that most marketing claims are bogus. It just means you have to ask a few more questions when shopping. And even when the product is legitimate, avoid falling into that other "eco" trap—buying it just because it's green.

PLANNING THE DETAILS

A green wedding requires thought and resourcefulness to plan, not necessarily more work or time. Many couples get creative to reflect their personalities and values, so they may make the extra effort to come up with handcrafted invitations or homemade centerpieces. But you don't have to be an artist or a policy wonk to build a model wedding. More vendors are offering the products you will want than ever before. (Try the Organic Trade Association's "The Organic Pages" at www.ota.com to start your search for retailers and suppliers.)

Your biggest challenge may be sorting through the offerings. Many products are green versions of the familiar—invitations of paper made with skins of garlic bulbs or the chaff of roasted coffee beans, for example—and you may want to try them out before you commit. Green products also come from online stores you may have never heard of—there is no green Macy's yet—so it may take you longer to settle on some vendors.

Some event planners specializing in green weddings also warn that you may still have to seek things out. You may not have any trouble finding organic food and drink, but you may have to look harder for a venue with an organic kitchen or one that recycles and composts its garbage.

And especially for a high-end celebration, "No one may be stocking the recycled vase of the quality you need," notes Venokur of dvGreen. But as you'll read below, it's all a question of balance.

ASSESSING THE COST

Depending on the product, you may pay a mark-up of 10, 20, 30 percent, sometimes more, for green."The market is still in its infancy, and it will continue to be more expensive, as long as there are limited choices with green," says Suzanne C. Shelton, president of the Shelton Group, an ad agency in Knoxville, Tennessee, focused on sustainability. The wedding planners I interviewed handled weddings with a budget of up to tens of thousands of dollars. But you can green your wedding at any budget and should aim for not only green but also lean. An organic menu, professional lighting with L.E.D. lights (light-emitting diodes use even less energy than compact fluorescent bulbs), bio-diesel–fueled generators—they may all require you to pay a premium. There are also the extras, such as if you plan to buy carbon offsets to compensate for the wedding's emission producers, from travel to the DJ.

The good news: Prices should even out as suppliers step up to meet the growing demand. "You'll see enough green products that the prices will be comparable to traditional products," Shelton says. And there are ways to get around some of the expenses. You can save on the

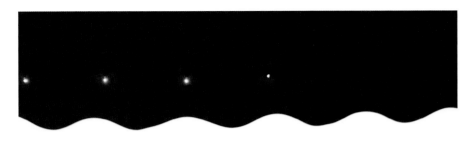

dress, for instance, by going for a second-hand gown. If you plan your wedding in a natural venue like a garden or park, you can save on flowers. Overall, though, Eric Fenster, owner of the green events company Back to Earth (www.BacktoEarth.com) in the San Francisco Bay Area, says that the price of the wedding is dictated by the complexity of the production.

"What makes weddings go from a low budget to high end is the amount of equipment, the sound, the lighting, the amount of staff you need," he says.

STAYING FLEXIBLE

While you may have no trouble finding most of what you need for a green wedding, you may have to adjust some of your green ambitions.

Take the issue of seasons. Margo Kaplan and Benjamin Gibson of Brooklyn, New York, who married before one hundred guests in June 2007 on the banks of New York's Hudson River, wanted seasonal ingredients for their meal, but those weren't available for tasting when they were shopping for caterers months before the wedding. For their summer wedding, they say, the caterer was able to offer a tasting only "of a few things" three weeks before, but the rest of the organic menu was locked in. "It's a leap of faith," says Margo. "It made us a little nervous."

Being willing to accept a few surprises is a must, the couple say. Sometimes the expected ingredients may not materialize because of shortages. Their assorted veggie succotash, for instance, ended up being mostly potatoes and corn. The lesson: Preparation is good, but when dealing with Mother Nature you must control your inner control freak. And there is a limit to what you can ask for. The couple wanted gazpacho, but tomatoes in their area were not flavorful at the time. The caterer offered a creative option: sweet peas.

It was delicious, they say, and so was the rest of the wedding menu.

TOP LEFT New York's Hudson River as viewed from the dance floor at the wedding of Margo Kaplan and Benjamin Gibson. **TOP RIGHT** The newlyweds make their way to the party. **BOTTOM LEFT** The groom breaks a glass following Jewish tradition. **BOTTOM RIGHT** The couple spend a few minutes alone on a wood swing under a willow tree.

A QUESTION OF BALANCE: COMPROMISES, TRADEOFFS, AND DILEMMAS

Fenster says some of his customers ask for "the most sustainable wedding ever created." They want to hold it during the day to avoid electric lighting. They want only acoustic music. They want an urban venue so guests can use mass transit. The food must be all organic, even vegan. And so on.

But many couples are not ready to compromise on certain elements. A fiancé may balk at giving in to his girlfriend's no-diamond request for the engagement ring (to avoid gems whose mining may have financed a war). Would people think him cheap? Would she later regret not having the rock?

Many brides resist parting with the idea of buying an expensive new wedding gown. (Of course, donating the dress afterward to an organization that will recycle the garment will go a long way toward making up for such a transgression.) The guest list is another nail-biting issue. How to leave out the coworker who sits next to you at the office? What about college roommates?

The wedding planner Danielle Venokur, who was designing her own green wedding and was looking at paring down a tentative list of two hundred loved ones, says you have to find a balance between green and what is personally important.

"It's one party," she says. "Feel good about it. Get the cake you want. And take the green message and apply it to the rest of your life."

Even when the choice is to go green all the way, dilemmas may arise. If no one in your area rents out the organic tablecloths you want, and they are only available for sale from an out-of-state company, wouldn't it be more sensible to avoid long-distance shipping and get something locally, even if it's not green? (The lowest footprint option, the people from Global Footprint Network say, is to rent the tablecloths—organic or not—from a place near home, to save both the emissions of transporting the tablecloths and the energy and resources that go

Candles perched on overhead planks bathe the reception in a warm glow.

into making them.) Roses from Ecuador may be sustainably grown but require long-distance shipping. You can get flowers from a nearby farm, but the farm heats its greenhouses, consuming lots of energy. Which is the more environmentally sound choice? (Plants and flowers that are grown locally and are in season, to avoid the heated greenhouse, says Global Footprint Network.)

"Use common sense and do the best you can with the information you have," says Andrew H. Darrell of the Environmental Defense Fund, an advocacy group. "Until there's an economic incentive that builds the environmental cost into the cost of goods we buy, we must simply do the best we can. And common sense suggests that trying to cut back on waste—wasted fuel, wasted packaging, wasted electricity—is a good thing for the planet *and* your wallet."

Dilemmas. Trade-offs. Unintended consequences. In these times of transition to a more responsible way of living, don't be afraid to lead. Research what you care about. And take it as far as you can.

Recycled chairs make for a playful décor.

GREEN MUSTS: ELEMENTS WITH THE MOST IMPACT

There is green, and green*er*. As you align your concerns for the Earth with your wedding budget, the choices available in the market, your guests' feelings, and your own dreams about the perfect wedding, you will strike balances and make trade-offs. But to benefit the environment the most, environmental experts I talked to advised focusing on:

1. **THE GUEST LIST.** I know. Touchy subject. But do you really have that many loved ones? The smaller the guest list, the smaller the impact on the environment. A greener alternative: leaving most guests at home and webcasting an intimate wedding instead. (See Chapter 2: The Venue.)

2. **THE VENUE.** Think about the carbon emissions your guests will produce by attending your nuptials. Choose a venue within a short ride for most guests. Avoid having guests fly to some exotic location like Jamaica for your vows on the sand. "If you're going to do a destination wedding, downsize the guest list and buy carbon offsets," says Alexandra Kennaugh, a spokeswoman for the Natural Resources Defense Council. But remember, carbon offsets should be the last resort—the better choice is to avoid emissions in the first place.

3. **FOOD AND BEVERAGES.** "Weddings do involve a lot of food and drink, and there is a huge difference between an all-vegan, all-organic banquet and a toxic meat fest," says John Talberth, director of the sustainability program for Redefining Progress, a public policy think tank. Believe or not, the livestock business, says the United Nations Food and Agriculture Organization, generates more greenhouse gas emissions than all forms of transportation combined.

4. **SOURCING.** We often hear that buying local is best, but the truth is that this may not always be the case. A fruit or a flower from a local farm means fewer travel-related carbon emissions. But some studies suggest that when emissions associated with production are also considered, a product traveling from afar may not necessarily be worse than the local alternative. The local farm may have consumed so much energy heating its greenhouse in the winter, for instance, that it counters the benefits from the close proximity to the buyer.

While the experts debate the food miles issue, many environmentalists say that, when in doubt, avoid the transportation emissions first. In other words, go local unless your own research tells you otherwise. "Nobody can do the exact math, but it's common sense that you should go with the local products," says Isabelle Silverman, a lawyer with the Environmental Defense Fund who specializes in green cities and air quality. "At the very least," she says, "you want to support the local economy."

5. **MONITORING CONSUMPTION.** Don't be tempted by eco labels. If you don't need it, don't buy it just because it's green.

CHAPTER 2

THE VENUE
WELCOME TO THE FARM

In looking for a venue, Kristi Papenfuss, 37, and Joshua Houdek, 33, of Minneapolis, Minnesota, wanted a natural setting for their afternoon wedding. But first, the venue had to mesh with their ambitious green goal: a zero waste event for 250 people where everything would be reused, recycled, and composted.

Couples typically pick nature for their green venue, but if you think outside the box you can find options beyond gardens, parks, or beaches. How about a working farm? Kristi, a teacher, and Joshua, a Sierra Club organizer, found their ideal spot at Gale Woods Farm (www.ThreeRiversParkDistrict.org) in Minnetrista, Minnesota, a farm in a 410-acre park that harvests its own produce and runs educational programs for teenaged "youth farmers."

The picturesque farm, which overlooks Whaletail Lake and pastures filled with livestock, served as the main décor for the couple's August 2007 wedding. That's not counting the solar panels from a rented solar power cart to juice up the sound system and a bluegrass band. "This was a neat thing to have as a visual," says Joshua.

With no dishwashing facilities at the farm, the bride and groom bought cups and tableware that were 100 percent compostable, made of potato, corn, and sugarcane byproducts. A catered, grilled dinner was local, organic, and mostly vegetarian. Table scraps could be fed to the farm's chickens and pigs, so no one had to cart away leftover food, and the farm recycles and composts on site. The venue was minutes from the Carver Park Reserve, where the newlyweds pitched a tent on their wedding night, alongside fifty of their guests.

For Kristi and Joshua, this was the perfect wedding—true to their values. "We didn't have a desire to have an elaborate wedding," explains Joshua. "By having a simple wedding, that is in itself more green."

Guests partake of an organic buffet at Kristi and Joshua's celebration at Gale Woods Farm, where the leftovers go to the pigs.

KEEPING IT GREEN FOR A THRONG:
AN ECO-CONSCIOUS COUPLE AND THEIR 250 GUESTS

Kristi Papenfuss and Joshua Houdek realized that to include all their loved ones would mean a huge party, not a very green option. But huge doesn't have to mean wasteful. They kept it simple and offered:

◎ Ceremony and reception at a farm with picnic table seating.

◎ Organic dinner, with choice of black bean veggie burger or organic Italian sausage "for people who would be freaked out by a veggie burger," Joshua notes.

◎ Compostable cups and tableware.

◎ Cupcakes instead of a cake, to avoid more plates and utensils.

◎ Beverages with dinner (no open bar but BYOB encouraged): Locally brewed beer from Finnegans, which donates all profits to local charities fighting poverty; Fair Trade wine and organic watermelon juice with locally grown melons.

◎ Folk dancing with four-member bluegrass band powered by a solar power cart (rented from the Minnesota Renewable Energy Society, which charges $35 a day, and available from other solar power companies).

◎ No ceremony programs or party favors.

◎ For accommodations, choice of hotel or camping with the bride and groom at Carver Park Reserve, just minutes from the venue (tents and sleeping bags provided).

Couples usually look for the venue with a well-defined picture in their mind—say, getting married with ocean waves lapping at their feet.

Day or night? Outdoors or indoors? Casual or elegant? Woods or beach? These are among the first questions couples usually ask themselves as they also look for a venue that is convenient and fits their budget. But what makes a venue green goes beyond the landscapes and views. This is the biggest item on the wedding budget—close to 50 percent if the food is included—therefore the one with most potential for waste, or savings. To keep that environmental footprint a dainty size, first develop a general idea of the setting and then stick to some basic guidelines to decide on the actual location (see "Be There!" on page 37). Small and simple is always greener. How about a home wedding in your backyard (or someone else's), where you control every element of the venue and can save money worth a down payment on your first home? Maybe a nicely landscaped backyard is not available, but couples find ingenious ways to balance their wishes with the green thing to do.

With a guest list of 150 people, Karin Ascot, 39, a German-English translator, and Patrick Van Haren, 40, an entrepreneur in renewable energy projects, split the crowd for a two-part celebration at Zilker Metropolitan

Karin Ascot and Patrick Van Haren exchange vows surrounded by 50 loved ones at Zilker Metropolitan Park in Austin, Texas.

Park in Austin, Texas, in the fall of 2006. The first part was a morning ceremony in one of the 350-acre park's gardens before some fifty guests, followed by a light lunch in a picnic area. "There were no chairs, no music," Karin says of the ceremony. "We just had a gathering. It was low-key, but it was very beautiful."

The celebration later continued on the picnic grounds for a 5 p.m. party and potluck dinner with the bigger group. With a singer and her acoustic guitar providing the musical backdrop, the newlyweds celebrated late into an evening filled with love and candlelight.

Outdoor venues like parks, vineyards, botanical gardens, and beaches have the advantage of providing their own natural décor. You may just need your bouquet and a few centerpieces for decorations. Daytime weddings save on electric power. Building-based venues, such as restaurants, rooftops, and hotels, offer amenities and the option of elegance.

If you demand as green as possible, you may want to see how the hotels, buildings, or churches you are considering measure up to standards and practices for energy efficiency, water conservation, and the like. For example, do they have lots of windows that let in natural light? Do they use appliances with the government Energy Star seal, which means they meet strict energy efficiency guidelines? Do they landscape with native plants that don't need as much irrigation?

For a guide to construction standards, check with the U.S. Green Building Council, whose LEED program (for Leadership in Energy and Environmental Design) certifies green buildings. Your venue may not be certified, but you can use the Council's green standards to see whether it has at least taken some action toward a greener path. Although the number of certified buildings was still small in 2008, it keeps growing. You can check which buildings are certified in your area at www.usgbc.org (click on LEED Project Directory). And yes, there are green churches and places of worship. The LEED directory already includes a few of them, led by the Methodist and Unitarian Universalist denominations.

But keep in mind that the emissions produced by the event itself are often slight compared to those generated by guests' travel, so think "location, location, location" first. (See Chapter 7: The Guests for more on guest travel.)

The botanical garden in Zilker Metropolitan Park in Austin, Texas, offered the greenest of venues to Karin Ascot and Patrick Van Haren.

When deciding on the wedding venue, environmental experts advise thinking about the weather. "Pick a time of the year when you don't need heating or cooling," says Kenneth P. Green, an environmental scientist and resident scholar with the American Enterprise Institute for Public Policy Research.

Also look for sites that:

◎ are close to most guests, to minimize the carbon emissions produced by air and car travel. For instance, you could throw two small wedding parties instead of one big one—say one on the East Coast and another on the West Coast—so that the two of you come to the guests, rather than the other way around. For that reason, destination weddings are not advisable, but if you must, make up for the travel by buying carbon offsets from a reputable company. (See Chapter 7: The Guests.)

◎ are close to public transportation, so that guests can leave their cars behind.

◎ accommodate both ceremony and reception, to avoid shuttling around venues. If the ceremony is in a church, plan the reception nearby.

◎ accommodate daytime events out of doors to avoid the need for lights.

◎ adhere to green practices, such as organic catering, recycling garbage, and using energy-efficient appliances. (For more on green building standards, check with the U.S. Green Building Council at www.usgbc.org.)

◎ offer or connect you with green services, such as organic flower vendors. The venue scores points if it provides those services itself to minimize the transport of supplies from different sources.

◎ do good. Some venues donate part of your fee to support environmental causes or are run by community, religious, and nonprofit centers that benefit directly from the fee. And don't forget artistic causes, like your favorite museum, gallery, or arts center.

The same advice applies for pre-wedding gatherings, such as the engagement party, the shower, the bachelor/bachelorette parties, or the rehearsal dinner. But since these gatherings are smaller than the wedding, finding the venue can be as easy as taking over an organic restaurant or your parents' home!

Another key question brides and grooms should ask, some wedding planners note, is "Who do I want to support?"

"Do you want the money to go to the Four Seasons Hotel or to the local community or a religious organization?" asks Corina Beczner, from Vibrant Events (www.VibrantEvents.net), a planner of sustainable events in the San Francisco Bay Area whose weddings are in the $25,000 to $75,000 range. "Giving back to the community and to people is as sustainable as preserving resources. Consider community centers and religious centers," Beczner suggests. "That money goes right back to the community."

Sometimes the venue literally hands over the money to a cause. Elizabeth Roberts, 38, and Dr. Michael McKnight, 39, of Brooklyn, New York, heard through a friend of a friend about Listening Rock Farm (www.ListeningRockFarm.com) in Wassaic, New York. The farm and environmental education center (including an area for producing biodiesel fuel) hosts a limited number of weddings to raise money for the Cary Institute of Ecosystem Studies in Milbrook, New York, which researches endangered animal populations like the pearly mussel, which lives in the river that runs through the property. Allan Shope, the architect and farmer who owns Listening Rock, says couples make a tax-deductible $10,000 donation to the Cary Institute for use of the venue, which can accommodate up to three hundred guests.

The cause sat well with Elizabeth and Michael, who had checked out standard venues in the Berkshires and found most unsatisfactory. "It felt a little soulless, like a wedding factory," says Elizabeth, an architect. "We thought, 'Where is this money going? Thousands of dollars for what?'"

Listening Rock Farm also had a train station within walking distance, important for a wedding with 135 guests. And it offered flowers from its own gardens. So on a beautiful afternoon in September 2007, Elizabeth and Michael held their sunset ceremony in a grassy field with a lush mountainside as a backdrop. The reception was in an old dairy barn with a gallery of pictures of "eco-heroes" such as American scientist and ecologist Rachel Carson and the French marine explorer Jacques Cousteau.

Before the ceremony, Shope thanked the guests and gave a short explanation of what they were supporting by being there. "The site was such a key part of the whole event," says Michael, an internist. "We felt it was good to have that back story before the ceremony began." Elizabeth admits that contributing to the health of mussels "is not something we set out to do, but it made sense when we heard of it." The couple extended their commitment to the mussels by becoming members of the Aldo Leopold Society, which supports the research and education projects of the Cary Institute.

"It's opened all sort of doors for us," she says.

OPPOSITE AND ABOVE Elizabeth Roberts and Michael McKnight get married in a grassy field at Listening Rock Farm in Wassaic, New York, where the fee for the venue, including an old dairy farm for the reception, goes to support an endangered mussel.

Some brides envision a ballroom straight out of a fairy tale for their wedding, but not Haily Zaki. Her idea of a perfect wedding celebration was to go camping!

"I always felt that weddings were a day of extravagance, and wasteful," says Haily, 28, a freelance writer and public relations consultant in Los Angeles who married Brian Tuey, 31, a video game designer, in April 2006. "Brian and I are outdoorsy, and we wanted it to be very much about what we wanted to do and who we were."

Haily and Brian found their venue at Sturtevant Camp, a nineteenth-century historic site in Southern California's San Gabriel Mountains run by the United Methodist Church at www.SturtevantCamp.org. Another website, www.CalPacCamps.org, lists sister campsites in Southern and Central California. Nonchurch members are welcome. Located above the cities of Sierra Madre and Arcadia in Los Angeles County, Sturtevant Camp can only be reached on foot, in a four-mile hike along with a pack train of mules that carry the food and luggage.

Yes, you read that right. Mules. And four miles of hiking. Uphill.

It helped that the thirty friends and coworkers who signed up for this three-day adventure were young, ranging in age from twenty-five to thirty-five. (The couple had already gotten the legal formalities out of the way at a courthouse and hosted a small gathering of relatives at their home the week before.) Still, some friends balked at the camping wedding idea—"I don't do camping," some

RSVP'd—until they were reassured that they would be sleeping in cabins with bunk beds, not tents.

So off they went on a Friday afternoon in single file through the woods to reach the camp nestled at 3,200 feet in a forest of big-cone spruce, canyon live oaks, and big-leaf maples. The swiftest reached the destination in 3½ hours—the slowest in 6. The guests then settled into the cabins built for 8 to 10 people—bathrooms were outside. The common areas included a dining hall with a kitchen

ABOVE AND OPPOSITE A 4-mile hike up to Sturtevant Camp in Southern California's San Gabriel Mountains, wood cabins, centerpieces of pine cones from the forest and…voila!—Haily Zaki and Brian Tuey accomplish what friends called "the coolest wedding" ever.

powered by hydro-electricity and propane, a lodge with a fireplace, and a croquet lawn. (Lights were out at 9 p.m., so the night owls in the group huddled around the fire until bedtime.)

The ceremony took place at dusk on a misty Saturday in the dining hall. Tables for a three-course, mostly organic meal of roast lamb, Waldorf salad, and berry cups were decorated with pine cones, leaves, and branches that were later returned to the forest. The bride donned golden flip-flops and an off-the-rack, $99 strapless dress with a tulle skirt that made her feel, she says, like the tooth fairy. Haily and Brian offered special vows to each other—his written by the female guests, hers written by the men. Then bride, groom, and best pals all took turns

after the ceremony flying through the treetops swinging from a zip line, in the dark.

For the hike back to their cars the next day, the mules carried trash, which had been separated for recycling by the camp.

"The idea of camping gave us three days—a lot more time for all of us to hang out and really get to know each other," says Haily. "In a hotel, it's four hours and you're done, and you're out $20,000."

Obviously, going off the grid is not for everyone. Did I forget to mention the bears and mountain lions roaming the area? But Haily says her friends declared the experience "the coolest wedding" ever. "It was like being kids again in summer camp," Haily says. "It was magical."

A plaque commemorating Haily and Brian's union stays behind at Sturtevant Camp.

GREEN BUILDINGS

Many brides want both magical and elegant, so with the green building trend has come the green formal venue. A good example is Barr Mansion and Artisan Ballroom (www.BarrMansion.com) in Austin, Texas, which bills itself as one of the first green special events venues in the nation. The mansion, which features an organic kitchen certified by Oregon Tilth, one of the organizations that certify vendors meeting United States Department of Agriculture organic standards, is surrounded by ginger-bread porches on three sides and has rooms suitable for cocktails and rehearsal dinners. Built in 1898 on seven acres, the property also includes a ballroom with a dramatic 40-foot-high glass facade.

Melanie McAfee, who has owned Barr Mansion with her husband, Mark, since 1980, says her biggest worry when she turned the kitchen organic in 2007, stepping up a move to more sustainable practices for the whole property, was perception. "We were worried that people would perceive it as an expensive thing and might not call us," she says.

McAfee's worries turned out to be unfounded. Demand, she says, has gone nowhere but up. "We're real competitive," she says. "We do not hear, 'Oh, golly, you're the most expensive place in town.'"

A crowd can spill over onto the grounds of Barr Mansion, a formal green venue in Austin, Texas, which can accommodate up to 800 guests.

Prices for the venue remained stable, McAfee says, because going green actually resulted in savings. The switch to organic food, for example, meant buying seasonal, which was cheaper than getting something like strawberries off-season from overseas. It also led to more exact shopping at local farms instead of buying food in bulk, some of which invariably went to waste. And the venue also saved money by starting to launder its own linens to avoid cleaning services that used bleach and "nasty chemicals," she notes.

Barr Mansion's prices are mostly determined by the size of the guest list—the more people, the cheaper the cost per person, McAfee says, but one thing to watch out for with venues is seasonal discounts. At Barr Mansion,

for example, it's sweltering hot in the summer and the trees are bare in January and February, so prices come down during those times.

Popular settings at Barr Mansion include a rose garden, a garden archway, and the ballroom. Most weddings are in the range of one hundred to two hundred guests, but the venue can handle up to eight hundred people on its grounds. The venue offers wedding planning services and can provide or connect customers with vendors of organic flowers, bio-diesel–fueled limousines, organic cotton tablecloths and hemp napkins, organic soy candles, and recycled glass containers for both candles and centerpieces.

But more significant are the steps Barr Mansion's owners have taken to green the entire venue, not just the weddings. They use geothermal power for cooling and heating and replaced freezers and other kitchen appliances with those carrying the Energy Star label for energy efficiency. They compost all food scraps for the mansion's rose garden. They send customers home with containers for leftovers that are made of corn and can be composted. The restrooms feature cloth napkins for the ladies and 100 percent recycled paper towels for the men. Even the staff's aprons and coats are made of organic cotton.

Attention to the last green detail has a goal: "We're trying to get to zero waste," says McAfee—meaning nothing from the venue would end up in a landfill.

THE VIRTUAL VENUE

You could always elope (what could be greener?) but there is a happy medium between a quickie wedding and saying your vows before two hundred of your closest friends: the cyber wedding, or streaming the ceremony live from its location to relatives and friends all over the world.

A wedding webcast may sound kind of fringe, but it allows you to cut down your guest list and still have all of your loved ones be part of the event (kind of). It is also the perfect option for your stuck-at-work friend in London or your ailing grandfather in Florida who can't travel.

Las Vegas wedding chapels have led this trend, factoring into their packages both free live broadcasts and an Elvis impersonator. But wedding videographers, dot-com companies, and even some cities have jumped on the bandwagon. One company, www.WebcastMyWedding.net, has technicians who can travel to your wedding to take care of the webcast (for $1,600 plus traveling expenses—in 2008 prices—for up to one hundred simultaneous viewers and thirty days of archived access.) The company also allows you to handle the webcast yourself for a fraction of the price ($595). The owner, Ariel J. Andres, who operates out of Texas and Georgia and does about thirty wedding webcasts a year, says all that couples need for the live streaming is a video camera, a laptop, and a high-speed Internet connection. After reserving a webcast channel, a couple can create their webpage and e-mail invitations with the time and date of the event so that guests know when to log on.

Another company, www.LiveVows.com, which mostly handles destination weddings in Destin and other beach locations in the Florida Panhandle, offers two-camera angles, streaming of both ceremony and reception and a DVD with the entire raw footage as part of its $1,800 webcast package. Other packages are available.

Who does this? Andres says his clients include a bride whose father in Germany couldn't travel to the States because of injuries he had suffered in a hunting accident. For them, Andres says, he set up a simulcast so that the father was able to give his daughter away from Europe on the webcast.

Another couple wanted to save money, so they had only eight relatives and close friends at their wedding in Santa Monica, California, but broadcast the beach ceremony to more than one hundred online guests. "They just wanted it to be small," he says, adding that the couple then went on to an intimate celebration with a few guests and then the honeymoon.

The advantages of the virtual approach: You save a ton in wedding expenses and there's nothing greener than downsizing and consuming less. The disadvantage: You may ruffle a few feathers. And don't expect gifts!

CHAPTER 3

THE GIFT REGISTRY

BEYOND POTS AND PANS

When Lesley Doerner and Jason Whyard registered at a department store for their April 2007 wedding, they chose Macy's, but they were interested in more than pots and pans. The store's wedding registry, operated in partnership with the wedding website WeddingChannel.com, promised to donate up to three percent of the amount guests would spend on gifts to a cause of their choice.

The Whyards, of Bergen County, New Jersey, have two cats and a dog, all adopted from shelters. "My husband is really into animals," Lesley, 28, who does fundraising for a Montessori school, says of Jason, 30, a store manager. "We have to go to the Bronx zoo every single year." So while getting their wedding presents, Lesley and Jason simultaneously directed donations to the Society for the Prevention of Cruelty to Animals.

"Some people who are lucky enough to have loads of money can have a charity registry," Lesley says. "We loved the fact that we could get dishes and at the same time money could go to a charity we cared about."

Registries have come a long way since the days when couples relied on them to equip a new home. With marriage coming at an older age—often in the late twenties or older—the bride and groom usually want to shed rather than hoard as they combine households. Wedding registries have stretched their scope accordingly; they can include honeymoons, theater tickets, wine, and power drills. Even banks have gotten into the act, setting up registries to help the newlyweds come up with the down payment for a new home.

Marriages in the United States number more than 2.2 million each year, says the Centers for Disease Control and Prevention. Multiply that by the number of wedding guests—each spending $50 to $150, according to a survey by TheKnot.com, a leading wedding website—and you have a bounty of consumer extravagance. Registries are worth billions of dollars a year, so it is no surprise that brides and grooms committed to rooting out waste in their lifestyles have extended their distaste for excess to their wedding presents.

Why ask for luxuries like a porcelain gravy boat from Tiffany if what you really need is help renovating your new home? Why not turn over the gift-fest to a charity or some other worthy recipient? Or get a subscription for a regular fresh-produce basket from a community-supported farm? Or to a green publication?

Lesley and Jason Whyard

GAG ME WITH A COMPOSTABLE SPOON:
HOW TO DEAL WITH THE RESISTANT GUEST

Good intentions aside, be forewarned: Your green wedding ideas may not fly with some guests. Your fashion-forward aunt may resent the farm venue. ("How am I supposed to not ruin my Jimmy Choos?") Your clownish coworker may mock your party favor. ("Seeds? What am I, a bird?)

At a wedding I attended, some well-heeled women avoided the already damp hand towels in the bathroom, where a sign read "There are paper towels if you prefer, but using these hand towels will save on waste." Outside, a table overflowed with wrapped gifts despite the couple's "no gift wrap" request.

To fend off rebellion, some etiquette experts suggest, explain the reasoning behind your decisions. Share with family members and guests your excitement about hosting a green wedding, and anticipate their questions. If your registry suggests donations or cash gifts, for example, guests are more likely to comply if you tell them where the money is going and why this is important to you.

But all you can do is ask, not demand, cautions Anna Post, a spokeswoman for The Emily Post Institute (www.EmilyPost.com) and author of "Emily Post's Wedding Parties." In other words, if your guests go their own way, suck it up.

Welcome Drinks

Please help yourself
to a tasty orange
welcome drink

(Contains Rum)

The cups are recyclable and Wildwood will compost the orange slices. Enjoy!

"Don't be angry or offended," Post says. "You have to consider people's feelings. Some people are trying to be respectful to you by wrapping the gift." Many couples instinctively know this. A few weeks before her October 2007 wedding in San Francisco, Stephanie Hibbert was philosophical about the honeymoon registry she expected to help finance a month-long trip to Thailand.

Hand Towels

In an effort to reduce our waste we have stocked the restrooms with hand towels (paper towels are still availabe if you prefer).

For sanitary reasons, Wildwood will throw-away everything disposed of in the restrooms. If you have cups or any other recyclables please bring them back to the recycling bins at the bar.

Thank You!

"I'm sure people will give what they want to give, and we'll appreciate it," she says. "If I get the vase, I'll get the vase. What can you do?" As it turns out, there are some things you can do:

◎ If you get the useless vase, say thank you "even if you hate it and hope your first kid breaks it," says Post. You can always try to exchange it, donate it, or re-gift it, although Post says the latter risks hurt feelings all around if the giver (to you) or the recipient (from you) finds out. Rebecca Black, an etiquette specialist at "Etiquette Now!"(www. EtiquetteNow.com) in California notes that getting rid of the gift only works if it's a generic item. Something unique, such as artwork, will be expected to make an appearance when your guest visits.

◎ If your parents roll their eyes at the organic menu, let your caterer do the talking. Eric Fenster of Back to Earth, the green events planning company in California, notes that parents of the bride and groom tend to want the traditional, such as a cocktail hour with classics like pigs-in-a-blanket and ten or so other heavy appetizers. But less can be more, says Fenster, who caters the cocktail hour with only four organic selections. "You can take four bites of something delicious and walk away remembering the food, rather than feeling overfilled," he says. "That's a huge conversation we have a lot."

◎ If you come within earshot of a snide remark—about, say, the organic beer—smile and move on or, better yet, says Black, "stop and ask, 'Do you have any questions about that?'"

"People don't get it, and that's fine," Black says. "Maybe they'll get it after somebody else does it. They may think you're not that silly after all."

Hosted Bar

Beer

Wine

Champagne

If you can, please bring your cup back and re-use it. And when you're done, please recycle it in the bins provided. Thanks for doing your part!

HOW A REGISTRY CAN DO GOOD

Couples who want their wedding spending to make a difference have become passionate about philanthropic registries. Do you want to rehabilitate prisoners, help disaster victims, support literacy programs, end world hunger, or stop global warming? Your registry can make you and your guests partners in a higher cause. Many charities and environmental nonprofits have set up their own registries to facilitate wedding gift donations. The World Wildlife Fund, for example, has a registry (www. WorldWildlife.org/weddings) for donations to the fund's conservation programs, including those to protect endangered species and help prevent over-fishing and deforestation. "Every dollar we receive helps fund projects all over the world, and it's a needed resource for us," says Kim Ritch, a spokeswoman for the organization.

How about a breathing gift? Heifer International (www.heifer.org), a nonprofit organization in Arkansas that works on projects to end world hunger, buys goats, sheep, and other animals for families in poor countries, to enable them to earn a sustainable income through agriculture. So your Uncle Charlie may very well buy a llama (price tag: $150) in your name and someone, somewhere, who depends on the llama for transportation or fleece for their ponchos, will benefit.

A poll by JustGive.org, a portal for charitable giving, found that many guests find donations a suitable wedding gift. But almost half the guests, the poll found, still threw in a small gift for the couple in addition to the donation. Let's call it a win-win.

GIFTS FOR THE SUSTAINABLE LIFESTYLE

Many couples are not forgoing wedding presents. It's just that instead of the crystal bowl, they're asking for the compost spinner. Bamboo tableware, patio furniture made of recycled milk jugs, recycled glass wine goblets, and other green items for the home can cost 20 to 30 percent more, so the registry may help you green your home faster.

Delilah Snell, owner of The Road Less Traveled in Santa Ana, California, says the higher prices reflect the living wages paid to workers, as in the case of Fair Trade products, and new products that have not yet achieved economies of scale. "You're investing in the technology of caring for the environment," Snell says.

Green stores like The Road Less Traveled have proliferated throughout the country and online, and you may find one around the corner. Many national stores popular for their registries, such as Crate & Barrel and Macy's, also stock green items. Some aggregator websites allow you to do one-stop shopping. One of the most popular, MyRegistry.com, allows couples to create a registry with any item they wish from any store, charity, or service in the world, in addition to cash gifts and items from offline stores. Payments go directly to individual vendors when guests buy a gift, and there's no extra charge to them or the couple (except a handling fee charged to the guest for cash gifts).

Ali Wood, 32, a New Yorker who had her May 2008 green wedding on a farm in Ohio, signed up through MyRegistry.com with Macy's as well as four green

Bamboo and steel table and side table, with matching chair. Fair Trade "La Chamba" cookware from Colombia. (All products from The Road Less Traveled)

A NEW GREEN ETIQUETTE:
HOW TO STEER GUESTS TO THE CAUSE

Couples hosting green weddings are rewriting traditional etiquette rules. They are suggesting guests offset their travel. They are donating to the Sierra Club in lieu of party favors. In a few cases, they are even e-mailing invitations. Etiquette experts sometimes disagree on the propriety of these measures, but many approve of the green wedding trend as a path toward a better future. "It's a wonderful thing," says etiquette specialist Rebecca Black, of Etiquette Now! "It's being polite to the planet. What can be more etiquette-y than that?"

"Green" and "manners" can go hand in hand just like the groom and bride, the experts say, as long as you keep one thing in mind: In your desire to do the right thing for the planet, don't forget about the comfort of those two-legged earthlings called "guests." "It doesn't

matter what type of wedding we plan—green, formal, or court house," says Black. "If we invite guests, we need to be good hosts."

It is considered a no-no to put registry information on the invitation—some guests may deem it the price of admission. Something else to avoid: Having your registry e-mail guests announcing that the registry is now open for business. "It is

as if you are saying, 'You are invited to my wedding to give me a special gift,'" notes Black. "It is very positive for a store's bottom line, but puts a greedy light on the couple." To spread the word about your registry, use your wedding website and good old word of mouth instead.

For invitations, the green way calls for reducing the use of paper and thus the preference for an electronic announcement among some couples. But the old etiquette, which calls for paper, still holds strong except for the most informal of weddings. "There's a gravity that you can't replicate on a computer screen," Anna Post, of the Emily Post Institute, says of both the paper invitation and handwritten thank-you note.

Many couples are using recycled paper for the invitations and the wedding website for all other communication, but how to

announce their website address? Put it on the save-the-date card, some experts suggest, or even better, in an e-mail blast.

Because invitations are strictly to announce your marriage, green messages such as "Recycle!" or "Be green!" violate etiquette. But since many invitations already come with

"Printed on 100% post-consumer recycled paper" anyway, that rule may already be passé.

Party favors are always optional, so you can easily skip them and not feel as if you're being rude. You can give away seeds or make donations to save the polar bear in the name of your guests. It's all your call.

But asking guests to offset the environmental impact of their travel is not acceptable, experts agree. It's just too much to force on guests on top of all the travel arrangements. "If we think logically and fairly, that means not burdening the guests with anything except 'Get here and be happy,'" says Black. Post suggests instead that you make room in your wedding budget to buy the carbon offsets for them.

Lastly, have a Plan B for guests without computers, like paper missives for grandma. Take account of people's feelings. If you know your older guests would appreciate a party favor, or a phone call or a visit to personally hear the wedding news, why not do it? Being thoughtful is what green is all about.

stores—www.TenThousandVillages.com (for Fair Trade products, including jewelry and home decor), www.3rliving.com (for green living), www.GreenFeet.com (for home furnishings), and www.GreenGlass.com (for recycled glassware). "You can register everywhere, and that's so cool," says Ali. She and her husband, Kevin Meeker, 31, wanted to support socially conscious companies, and were able to do it without having to juggle multiple registries at the same time.

ABOVE LEFT Ali Wood and Kevin Meeker's registry lists products designed from sustainable and recycled materials.
ABOVE RIGHT The couple shares their first moments as newlyweds in front of an "altar" created with items from around the family farm that served as their venue, including an old iron wagon from around the turn of the century that belongs to Kevin's grandfather.

ASKING FOR THE UNORTHODOX GIFT

The sky is the limit for useful wedding presents and the registries that accommodate them. Karin Ascot used the registry for a future need: items for a baby. She and her groom, Patrick Van Haren, suggested gift certificates so they could stock up on hemp diapers and organic cotton baby towels for the child they were planning to have soon after the wedding.

Other couples sign up with honeymoon registry websites run by travel companies, hotel chains, and other vendors that function just like the traditional registry. You itemize each honeymoon expense—air fare, hotel nights, dinners, tours—just the way you would do with kitchen appliances or towels. But watch out for hefty service fees, and compare prices for the tours offered. Sometimes you may be able to travel cheaper if you just collect the money and arrange the honeymoon yourself.

Kelly Nichols and Alan Puccinelli of Danville, California, registered with Backroads, the active travel company, to go on a bike trip along the Dalmatian Coast of Croatia. They needed $10,000 to make it happen, so on their website they explained: "It's not a traditional way to honeymoon, but we can't think of any way we'd rather travel together." The couple said pedaling together was their ideal romantic getaway, "so if any of you were so inclined," they wrote, "you could donate to our adventure!"

Their guests paid for ten percent of the trip but most ignored the honeymoon pitch. "I felt like a lot of my friends donated to the trip, and the older guests still want to get you china," Kelly says. "We didn't register for china, and we still got some crystal bowls!"

In fact, guests sometimes say, "No, no, no!" and you must prepare for rebellion (See "Gag Me with a Compostable Spoon" on page 50). Margo Kaplan and Benjamin Gibson, of Brooklyn, New York, who got married before one hundred guests in June 2007, say only two guests chose a wedding present in the form of a donation to their charity registries, which included Doctors Without Borders and Hurricane Katrina Relief Fund (even though the donations were fully tax deductible). A few more guests donated anywhere from $20 to $100 to the registries, but only in addition to a traditional gift from the couple's registries at Bed Bath & Beyond and other stores.

Kelly and Alan, through their wedding website, asked their guests "if you ship gifts, opt for no wrapping paper." "Some people gave us gifts in grocery bags or put them in a shoe box or wrapped them in newspapers," she says. "They ran with it. There were some people that thought that was funny and went the extra mile." But half of the shipped presents came wrapped, or in a box.

"It's literally a box within a box," Kelly notes. "I just wish it wasn't even an option."

GIMME, GIMME:
REGISTRIES FOR EVERY TASTE

Here's how to find the registries that can help the poor, support green vendors, and send you off on the honeymoon.

Popular green stores:

◎ Gaiam.com

◎ Greensage.com

◎ BranchHome.com

◎ UncommonGoods.com

◎ VivaTerra.com

◎ GreenandMore.com

◎ Global Exchange Online Store at www.gxonlinestore.org

For charities, check out www.JustGive.org, a San Francisco nonprofit that aims at increasing charitable giving across the United States. The I Do Foundation at www.IDoFoundation.org gives a portion of the price of gift purchases (up to ten percent) to your chosen cause, as does WeddingChannel.com (up to three percent). Also try CharityGiftCertificates.org. and the registries of individual organizations like the World Wildlife Fund (www.WorldWildlife.org) and Heifer International (www.Heifer.org).

MyRegistry.com is a popular one-stop-shop portal to thousands of retailers and services. Also try www.LocalHarvest.org to find community supported agriculture farms in your area for subscriptions to fresh food, and FairTradeFederation.org for fair trade products.

GIFT WRAP AND PACKAGING

In a nod to green sensibilities, some vendors are using packaging made of recycled materials and avoiding the plastic "popcorn." If you get a box that looks a little banged up, your vendor may be reusing boxes as a green measure. If you get the smallest box possible, your vendor may be trying to minimize the packaging.

I checked with GreenandMore.com, an online retailer of eco-friendly home goods, to find out how one green vendor handled registry gifts. Margie Brenner, one of the company's executives, told me Green and More uses recyclable cardboard boxes made from 100 percent post-consumer content and reused paper fillers, rather than those made of Styrofoam or plastic bubble wrap. There's no gift wrap option "because it's just not a green thing to do," she says. The company suggests the use of stylish reusable bags instead.

More than one bride told me she wished more registries gave customers the option of paying extra to offset the carbon emissions produced from shipping orders. Brenner says Green and More was not there yet, but the company had a program called "spare change for the environment," which allows customers to round up their total order to the next dollar or more at checkout, say from $82.50 to an even $83 or higher, and donate the change to environmental organizations like Oceana, which campaigns to protect the world's oceans. Up to 40 percent of customers choose to donate, Brenner says, and some even give as much as an extra $15.

Kelly and Alan give the groomsmen reusable grocery bags and other unwrapped gifts.

GREEN WEDDING 101: HOW TO INSPIRE, NOT PREACH

Many couples say they try to avoid being ostentatiously green, but this is tricky when you are also trying to inspire your guests to follow your lead. The wedding offers a chance to educate friends and relatives not yet clued in to terms like "post-consumer recycled paper," but how can you do this without a Power Point presentation between courses?

Kelly Nichols and Alan Puccinelli of California used their wedding website to show "How we're being eco-friendly." It explained that the venue composted on-site. It mentioned the organic menu and the bio-degradable wood stir-sticks for drinks. And under "What can you do?" it included tips such as "ride our chartered bus" and "wear a dress you already own."

For guests who don't go near a computer, Kelly and Alan highlighted some of the wedding's environmental features during the reception with signs such as: "Hosted drinks—beer, wine, and champagne. Please reuse your cup when you can, and recycle it when you're done."

At the wedding of Joshua Houdek and Kristi Papenfuss in Minnesota, the portable cart with solar panels that powered the sound system became a conversation piece. At the wedding

of Elizabeth Roberts and Dr. Michael McKnight at a farm in upstate New York, the owner of the venue spoke for ten minutes before the ceremony about the farm's ongoing research to save the endangered pearly mussel.

The wedding planners and etiquette experts I spoke to had mixed views about using the wedding as a platform to spread the green message. Events planner Danielle Venokur of dvGreen in New York says she discourages clients from doing things like placing cards on the table announcing carbon offsets. "I just think it's a little tacky to say your transportation was offset. So what?" she argues. "I don't try to dissuade them from telling people, but I try to dissuade them from making it a focus."

Etiquette experts agree that the focus should remain on celebrating, not teaching. Some warn that guests may be put off by too earnest an effort. A little card explaining the party favor of flower seeds is fine. But anything that may come across as showing off or flaunting your green cred is a big no-no.

Nevertheless, the opportunity to reach a captive audience can't be missed, says Dr. Meg Lowman, a professor of biology and environmental studies at New College of Florida and vice president for education at the Ecological Society of America. At her own wedding, she decided to give her guests a novel party favor—"insect candy" consisting of real crickets embedded inside lollipops and chocolate, from www. Hotlix.com. Dr. Lowman says she wanted to spread the notion that people in many countries eat insects, which she notes are a much more sustainable source of protein than, say, beef. "If you have a little card explaining why you did it, it really sticks," she says. "People love a story."

Many guests agree. Tammy Ehrenfeld, an advertising executive in Los Angeles who sat through the talk about the endangered pearly mussel at the New York wedding, says she didn't mind it at all. "He told us something new," she says. "It was thought-provoking."

CHAPTER 4

THE DRESS
A HEMP GOWN, YOU SAY?

For a wedding at the Architecture and Design Museum in Los Angeles one Friday evening in the summer of 2007, the bride wore paper—silky, shiny, translucent (and double layered!). The dress was long, in a classic A-line, and it was held together in the back by a red sticker in the shape of a heart. It looked like you could take it off after one evening, clump it into a ball, and throw it in the recycling bin with the morning papers.

Kay Moonstar makes a statement with a silk paper gown by Finnish designer Tuija Asta Järvenpää. "It felt right," said the bride, with a bouquet of succulent plant and crystal by Los Angeles botanical designer Krislyn.

Which was the point. A disposable wedding gown makes the statement that what makes the dress valuable is the experiences you have in it, not whether it has hand-beaded Swarovski crystals or was designed by Monique Lhuillier. This particular creation was part of a contemporary "Design as Cultural Interface" exhibit from Finland touring the United States, and it starred in a real wedding ceremony at the A+D museum, between artists Kay Moonstar and Stephen Platt.

"This is to push people to start thinking 'what's the value of an object?'" says Tuija Asta Järvenpää, a designer in Helsinki who sells her paper wedding dresses for $2,000 to $3,000. "Why is it that we have all these objects around us? Could we live with less?"

Most eco-conscious modern brides are not ready to say their vows in a paper bag, even a glamorous one, but they *are* looking for practical alternatives to the traditional, and expensive, gown. They are buying dresses they can wear again. They are turning to organic fabrics that were not processed with harmful chemicals and bleaches. Sometimes they are borrowing a dress from a former bride or buying a used one.

Why? Because too often the wedding gown just sits there, out of sight, never to be enjoyed again. Actress Katherine Heigl couldn't have put it better. "I loved my wedding dress," she told *People* magazine two months after her December 2007 nuptials. "And now it's in a ball at the bottom of a garment bag."

Fashion's impact on the environment can be harsh. It comes in the form of the pesticides used to grow crops like cotton, in the chemicals and dyes used to turn raw materials into textiles and garments, and in the wastefulness inherent in trying to keep up with fleeting fads. This is not counting transportation-related pollution.

"Some people get a fabric in China, have it embroidered in France, sewn in Italy, and ship it here," says Linda Loudermilk, a pioneering designer of high-end sustainable clothing in Los Angeles. "The footprint is just horrendous." Loudermilk says she looks for local fabrics or combines shipments from other places to cut down on carbon emissions.

For the environmentally aware bride, the key issue is waste. Many say they just don't see the point of spending a small fortune, often $2,000 or more, on a dress that will outlive its function in a matter of hours. "People preserve it and keep it under the bed for fifty years," notes Kelly Nichols. "It's just a piece of clothing."

But many brides tend to be set on a dream gown, and it's hard to get them to budge. "If brides have an idea of what they want to look like that day, it's hard to fight that," says Corina Beczner, the green events planner in San Francisco.

But even these brides (you?) can check out alternatives like a gown in eco-fabrics such as hemp, a prolific fiber that may be suitable for a beach or park wedding; a vintage or heirloom gown; a multiple-wear evening gown; or even a borrowed gown.

Don't knock it. Read on.

"Wind Spirit Dress" in organic cotton gauza by Linda Loudermilk, Luxury eco™.

THE REUSABLE WEDDING GOWN

A sure sign that the reusable concept had caught on came one Sunday morning in December 2007 when I opened my *New York Times* to the "Vows" section in Sunday Styles and came across the line: "The bride wore recycled Vera Wang." The bride was none other than Congresswoman Gabrielle Giffords, 38, a Democratic representative from Arizona, who had borrowed the gown from a friend to marry Mark E. Kelly, 43, a NASA astronaut and Navy pilot from New Jersey. The A-line silk gown with spaghetti straps required only minor alterations. Their wedding, of course, was green. "I was excited to wear a recycled dress," Rep. Giffords told me a few months after the wedding. "For me it was ideal. I felt great." She explained: "All my life I've known women who store their dress, or their mother's wedding dress, in a corner of their closet with the fantasy that someone is going to wear it and that never happens. The wedding is a commitment of two people standing before friends and family. It's about the experience of being there, it's not about the dress you're wearing. To spend hundreds or thousands of dollars on a dress you'll never wear again to me it's a mistake. To make a statement with a (new) dress defeats the purpose of what I was trying to achieve at my wedding."

Kelly Nichols, 26, who got married in the fall of 2007, says she first thought of borrowing her wedding dress from her older sister, who had married five years earlier. She did not consider new, even in an eco-fabric like hemp, she says, because "hemp is still harvested and

made, but if you borrow it there's no resources spent."

But her sister's dress did not fit her body type well, and she was not about to compromise on looking good. Her next step was to go to stores that sold used dresses, but she found the styles old-fashioned and something the bride's mother, not the bride, would wear. "They were still $4,000," she notes.

Kelly then moved her hunt over to eBay and Craigslist after trying on styles at a bridal store and deciding she wanted a strapless, A-line dress. All she cared about once she settled on a style, was that the dress come with good karma. On Craigslist, she ran into one glitch—not every dress advertised was used. Many sellers, Kelly discovered, were getting rid of a brand new dress after finding another gown they liked better. And on eBay, a lot of offers came from stores rather than individuals.

But two months into her search, Kelly found her dress, a Maggie Sottero design. She got it for $300 from "this sweet woman named Lisa" who told her, "There's no bad karma here. I'm still married and I'm pregnant, so we're cleaning out the closet."

Why did she let go of an idea so many brides still hold on to—to wear a dress of their own to treasure as a keepsake and even pass on to future generations? "If you're really going to keep it for your kids it's OK, but chances are it'll be very out of style," Kelly says. "Everybody acted like it was a big compromise, but I found the dress I wanted and I was happy."

THE PARTY DRESS REVISED

Many brides do insist on a new dress, however. Those who want a new dress but are still mindful of avoiding waste often buy a non-bridal style, something they could wear again at a party or the opera without looking like a runaway bride.

Some brides customize the dress to infuse it with more meaning. For her 2007 pirate-themed green wedding (yes, pirate!) at Treasure Island in San Francisco Bay, Stephanie Hibbert, 39, an organic chef, bought a long, inexpensive strapless white satin dress with black bead embroidery on the bodice. Then she asked the women in her family and some of her girlfriends to contribute a piece of black lace from a garment that was special to them. She ended up with twenty-five pieces to attach to the skirt. (For more on her wedding see Chapter 8: The Reception.)

"Every time somebody gave me a piece, there was a great story behind it," Stephanie says. "Two of my friends have been in bands, and they gave me pieces of clothing they wore on stage."

Karin Ascot of Texas got her ivory-colored, V-neck, sleeveless dress for her wedding at David's Bridal (www. DavidsBridal.com). It was a bridesmaid's dress, for $200, and Karin planned to dye it for future wear.

Karin Ascot dons a silk and chiffon bridesmaid's dress from David's Bridal for her wedding in a park. "I could dye it and wear it again," she said of her purchase.

THE GREEN RUNWAY

When it comes to The Dress, green can be fabulous new or fabulous second-hand, if you consider:

◎ Borrowing the gown that a friend, sister, or another relative wore at her wedding. If you are out of luck, search online for "wedding dress rentals" and check out the possibilities.

◎ Shopping Craigslist and eBay for second-hand or vintage. Some tailors specialize in making vintage gowns fit or look more hip with alterations. Also try used designer gown websites like www.PreownedWeddingDresses.com.

◎ Buying your dress from a charity such as the Making Memories Breast Cancer Foundation (www.MakingMemories.org), which grants the last wishes of breast cancer patients and sells both used and brand new gowns, some from well-known designers.

◎ Buying an evening gown you can wear again at any dressed-up event.

◎ Spending little. For her camping wedding celebration in California, Haily Zaki donned golden flip flops and an off-the-rack, $99 strapless dress with tulle skirt. (Since her 2006 wedding, the dress has been her Halloween tooth fairy costume.)

◎ Going with eco-fabrics for off-the-rack or custom-made gowns, as well as lingerie. Online retailers sell wedding gowns and men's suits in hemp, bamboo, tencel, and peace silk (which allow the silkworms a full life cycle). Check out Conscious Clothing (www.GetConscious.com) in Santa Fe, New Mexico, and Threadhead Creations (www.ThreadheadCreations.com) in Knoxville, Tennessee. For couture in organic wool, soy silk and other eco-fabrics, try designers like Linda Loudermilk (www.LindaLoudermilk.com) and Elisa Jimenez (www.Elisaj.com). For robes, camisoles, bras, and other lingerie in eco-fabrics, click on "Greenleaves" at www.Figleaves.com, one of the intimates retailers that carry a green line.

ECO-FABRICS

For brides who find it difficult to compromise on the traditional wedding gown, no matter how earth-friendly the alternatives, the fashion industry has come up with a tantalizing solution: eco-fabrics.

Today, it is possible to wear a blazer made out of cork over an organic cotton T-shirt with jeans dyed with persimmon fruit. Similarly, a bride can find a wedding gown made out of hemp, bamboo, wool, or soy silk. What makes a fabric eco? Leslie Hoffman, Executive Director of Earth Pledge, a nonprofit group that promotes sustainable technologies and works with the fashion industry, says eco in fabrics aims at reducing the environmental impact of "growing fiber or producing it in a lab or factory, processing it into a textile, coloring or printing it, cutting and sewing, packaging and shipping, laundering and disposing of it after all uses." Companies may work at limiting their energy and water use and pollution, the fibers may come from renewable sources, or they may be harvested and processed free of chemicals and pesticides.

Far from the crunchy granola image of the past, organic fabrics—as well as reclaimed fabrics from other garments—have made it into the salons of couture designers like Loudermilk, Stella McCartney and others who show their latest creations—sexy, slinky, and sophisticated—on runways in New York, Los Angeles, and London.

Designer Elisa Jimenez, 42, a contestant on season 4 of *Project Runway*, makes dresses for the bride and bridesmaids out of paper, organic cotton, organic silk,

Elisa Jimenez models her "Radiant Illusion" wedding dress made of Ingeo fiber.

and Ingeo, a fiber made from corn. "You basically can have fabrics that can compete with micro-fiber and the sensuality of it," says Jimenez, who custom makes wedding dresses for $875 and up. "She can have a wedding dress that looks like any other gorgeous couture wedding dress. Being conscientious about what you do is the new luxury item, the new status symbol."

One of the pioneers in the "luxury eco" movement is Linda Loudermilk, who launched her first eco-clothing line for women in 2003 and in just a few years added sustainable luxury lines for men's clothing and for jewelry, furniture, and bedding. (Hollywood A-listers like Adrian Grenier, from the HBO show *Entourage*, wear her suits.) For wedding gowns that retail in the $8,000 range, Loudermilk uses lightweight organic wool, sasawashi (a mix of bamboo leaves and Japanese Kumazasa plants) and soy silk, regarded as the cashmere of vegetable fabrics. And she is constantly helping develop new fabrics.

Loudermilk says her guiding principle as she works with fiber manufacturers to test new fabrics is: "What's an excess material that we can use?"

She also uses only nontoxic dyes, although she concedes some eco-fabrics don't take color well. "The red may be a little lighter," she says. But she vouches for their durability. "You care for it like you care for anything else," she says.

One drawback for most consumers is price. Eco-chic can cost about 20 percent more than other fabrics, and some materials, like organic silk, can be five times as expensive as non-organic, Loudermilk says. Prices should come down as the fabrics become more popular with designers and more manufacturers use sustainable materials, she says, but in the meantime avoid the eco-fake. "You're not to trust anything that says natural," she warns. "It's a completely bogus label. You can trust certified organic."

OTHER ATTIRE

Grooms have it easier—a rented tuxedo and they are good to go, right? But both grooms and groomsmen are reaching into their closets for their favorite suits or taking the opportunity to buy a nice outfit that they will wear again.

The green option for bridesmaids is also a dress they already have or that they will wear again. Imagine their thrill at not being asked to invest in something impractical or, even worse, bridesmaid-y. Some brides may set parameters for their bridal party, such as coordinating dress length or color. Another option is what my bridesmaids did for my wedding in 2005: They found a great dress in the Banana Republic Spring catalog and ordered it in their favorite colors, once again ensuring the dress would become part of their wardrobe. My sister, more frugal than contrarian, wore a dress she already had with no affinity to the others other than its knee length. She stood out, but everyone thought it was done on purpose since she's my only sister.

Some brides, like Kelly Nichols, feel it is important that the bridesmaids look coordinated. "For me the pictures were a really big deal," she says. "I wanted photos that I loved. I wanted bright colors. I felt being a bridesmaid is an honor, and I wanted them to stand out." So while her own dress was second-hand, her bridesmaids wore brand new.

OPPOSITE Kelly Nichols achieves a "something old, something new" look for the bridal party: the bride wears recycled, the bridesmaids brand-new.

ABOVE A borrowed Vera Wang gown goes beautifully with the groom's military uniform at the wedding of Congresswoman Gabrielle Giffords and U.S. Navy Commander Mark E. Kelly.

BYE-BYE DRESS

In the mid-2000s, a trend caught on among some brides—trashing the wedding dress for artistic pictures that may show the bride swimming in the gown—as in backstroke—or lying on dirt in grungy settings. Needless to say, no matter how hostile you may feel toward the dress by the end of the wedding, destroying it is not green.

Brides can make their wedding dress reusable by selling it, or even better, donating it to a charity that can recycle it to raise funds for a cause. (Eco-friendly dry cleaners can also now be found.) Look for programs in your area, like www.FairyGodmothersInc.com, that recycle wedding dresses into prom dresses for low-income high school girls.

The Making Memories Breast Cancer Foundation will be happy to take your gown and sell it at one of its more than thirty wedding dress events around the country. The money goes toward granting the last wishes of terminally ill breast cancer patients nationwide. You can buy your gown, used or brand new, at the same events. At the dress sale I attended in Anaheim, California, in February 2008, rack after rack of dresses—more than one thousand of them in white, beige, burgundy, and other colors—sold for $99 to $799, despite a value of up to $8,000.

"Families go to Disney World together for the last time, or have second honeymoons," Fran Hansen, one of the founders of the program, told me of the wishes each dress helps make a reality.

Jimenez says brides have other options to dispose of the dress in a thoughtful way. The removable train can be a blanket for your first child, she says. You could also frame it and make it a piece of art. If a paper dress, Jimenez says, "I'd have all my guests sign it [which is what Kay and Stephen did during their museum wedding reception in Los Angeles] and then frame it."

After her wedding, Kelly sent Lisa, the woman whose wedding dress she had bought, a picture of herself as a bride. She felt a connection with the woman, and it made her feel the dress was special. But the gown was headed back to Craigslist, hopefully for another twirl on the dance floor at another green wedding.

ACCESSORIES

So now that you have your dress (and the groom his suit), you need shoes and jewelry, and maybe a veil or tiara? You can follow the same green rules (something borrowed, recycled, or vintage) with most accessories and even find a few more options, such as artisan jewelry and socially conscious shoes. Here are a few ideas:

SHOES. MINK Shoes (www. MinkShoes.com) in Beverly Hills sells non-leather shoes for women, handmade in Italy with natural or "scientifically engineered" materials like cork, denim, linen, and faux fur. Charmoné Shoes (www. Charmone.com) in Massapequa, New York, carries animal-free evening shoes suitable for

the bride and bridesmaids. Also check out actress Natalie Portman's line of vegan shoes at www.TeCasan.com and the cruelty-free footwear for men and women at www. MooShoes.com

JEWELRY. Some brides go to Craigslist.org for used shoes, jewelry, headpieces, and other accessories. Also check out companies with Fair Trade inventory like World of Good (www. OriginalGood.com), which sells the crafts of artisans from all over the world.

You can also rent expensive accessories through websites like www.ImOverItOnline.com, www.BagBorroworSteal.com, and www.BlingYourself.com.

THE RING

When Katie Malouf of Washington, D.C., thought about diamonds, she could only see red, as in blood. "How awful that for a symbol of your love—some person practically died to get it for you," she says.

There has been much debate about "conflict diamonds," or diamonds from regions—usually in Africa—ravaged by wars. As portrayed so vividly in the Leonardo DiCaprio movie *Blood Diamond*, the gems have at times been mined illegally or used by rebel groups to finance conflicts that have claimed many thousands of lives and displaced millions of people. Objectionable practices are also found in places like India, where some diamonds are polished by children.

Diamonds still carry a powerful magic for many couples. So what should they do? For starters, grooms should find out how

their loved one feels about the ring. In Katie's case, her fiancé, Joe Bous, had been set on giving her a diamond. Traditions, after all, are hard to break. But she asked for, and got, a pink sapphire for her engagement ring instead.

"Joe was really bummed," says Katie. "He's a little bit more traditional. He wanted a diamond

so other people would know I was engaged because other rings are not as recognizable."

But couples who insist on a diamond can still buy one with a clear conscience. Online retailers like BrilliantEarth. com sell diamonds from Canada and guarantee that their products are "ethically mined, cut, and polished"—in other words, conflict-free. Clean diamonds can also be obtained from other places, even in Africa, but buyers need to be assertive and ask retailers for their policy on conflict diamonds and a written guarantee from suppliers. The guarantees come from the diamond industry's own voluntary tracking system (known as the Kimberley Process), and it's not perfect because of problems with oversight. But by requesting one, consumers are sending the message that this is an issue they care about. (For more consumer information, check with the human rights group Global Witness at www.GlobalWitness.org.)

One attractive alternative is going vintage and looking for antique diamonds—maybe to be found within your own families—that can be remounted. Stephanie Hibbert, of San Francisco, found her white gold ring with a solitaire diamond in a pawn shop. Her wedding ring, white gold encrusted with small diamonds, came from the same set. "Some people may think this is a little lowbrow, but the concept of reusing a ring was a really good idea," she says.

Many couples are ditching the diamond altogether and looking for a different kind of rock. For her engagement ring, Margo Kaplan, of New York City, went for a ruby in an antique platinum band from an antiquities store. "I wanted something with history," she says. Her wedding ring, a gold band with small sapphires, belonged to her maternal grandmother. "I liked it, and I didn't see the point of buying more jewelry," she says. "It has sentimental value. I remember it from when I was a little girl."

Look also for recycled gold and platinum. Gold and platinum mining has its own issues, including water pollution and displacement of communities. A number of retailers, including Tiffany & Co., have joined an international campaign for responsible gold mining operations. Check out www.NoDirtyGold.org for a list of supporting retailers.

And talk about sentimental value—Greenkarat.com has a registry through which you can collect old gold jewelry from your friends and family and melt it down to make your rings. Other options for both brides and grooms and the places to start out your search include:

◎ colored gemstones (www.LeberJeweler.com)

◎ synthetic or lab-made diamonds (www.ApolloDiamond.com)

◎ handcrafted wooden rings from salvaged lumber (www.etsy.com)

◎ sustainably mined gold and platinum jewelry (www.sumiche.com)

OCTOBER

THOUSAND AND

O'CLOCK IN THE EVENING

The Calistoga Ruins

CALISTOGA, CALIFORNIA

COCKTAIL ATTIRE

CHAPTER 5

THE INVITATION
WE'RE GETTING MARRIED!

For their wedding invitations, Margo Kaplan and Benjamin Gibson of Brooklyn, New York, stuck with the tried-and-true formula—something old and something new. Margo, 28, a civil rights lawyer, and Ben, 33, an associate art director, turned to the Internet to create a wedding website to give their guests information that used to be delivered in an envelope. "Save the date" notices traveled by electronic mail. Travel arrangements, hotel accommodations, the gift registry, and other details were posted online. Even invitations to the rehearsal dinner were emailed.

Mr. and Mrs. Jon Adams
request the honour of your presence
at the marriage of their daughter

Tracy Lynn
to
Christopher Priest McCurry

On Sunday, the twenty-third of January
Two thousand and ten
five o'clock in the evening

The Courtyard at Lake Lucerne
211 North Lucerne Circle East
Orlando, Florida

Reception immediately following ceremony

But to formally invite one hundred loved ones to their June 2007 wedding, Ben and Margo made a trip to an old-fashioned stationery store. For the formal invitations, only paper would do.

This is sentimental territory. The invitation is where your family names come together for the first time—where your union becomes tangible. And there are those who love you and will want to hold on to the wedding invitation as a memento.

Brides like Margo prefer paper for practical reasons as well. Not everyone has an e-mail address or is familiar with how to use the Internet, especially those in older

An invitation made of recycled cotton fiber from eInvite. com's Cast Paper Art line.

generations, she says. And people are more likely to respond to paper invitations, because they are more formal, less ephemeral. "You know what paper invitations will look like to every recipient, whereas electronic ones can show up strange or garbled on other people's computers," Margo says.

And, she noted, "We were a little more confident that paper invitations would reach the recipient and not be lost, unlike e-mails."

Still, the paper industry is in need of scrutiny. Natural forests have been replaced by tree farms for paper production. Mass amounts of energy go into turning those trees into paper. Large amounts of water are required to bleach the paper. Toxins are released in paper bleaching.

Pollutants known as volatile organic compounds, or V.O.C., are released by inks made with petroleum. And in the end, though over half the paper we consume is recovered for recycling, vast amounts of paper still end up in landfills, creating methane, a greenhouse gas, as it breaks down.

"Paper is one of the biggest contributors of greenhouse gas emissions in the manufacturing process," says Joshua Martin, a spokesman for the Environmental Paper Network, an advocacy group.

Some couples save on both pollution and expenses by sending wedding invitations electronically, but wedding etiquette experts agree: Except for the most informal of weddings, the personal touch of paper is a must. And an e-mailed thank-you note? Perish the thought! (See more on etiquette in Chapter 3: The Gift Registry.)

Even Amy Ruocco, founder and president of WeddingWindow.com in Massachusetts, which helps couples create their own wedding websites, draws the line. That is why she partnered up with the online stationery retailer eInvite.com in 2008. The two companies link to each other to offer dozens of coordinated looks—in color schemes and designs like "floral," "stars & confetti," and other motifs—between the site's templates and eInvite's paper products. The paper in eInvite's green product line is made of recycled fibers such as cotton and abacá (banana plant). The company offers vegetable-based inks and envelopes made of 100 percent post-consumer waste paper (see "Paper: What's in a Name" on page 83).

"There's a place for everything," Ruocco says. "When you're trying to show appreciation or introduce something, that's when you do the physical connection."

Wedding websites like those offered at WeddingWindow.com keep guests informed without the need for paper correspondence.

PAPER: WHAT'S IN A NAME?

When shopping for paper, you will come across terms like "tree-free," which means it is not virgin paper made from wood pulp. Paper can also be "recycled" or made from scraps in the paper-making process. It can be "100 percent post-consumer waste recycled," meaning made from paper that has already gone one round with consumers, like the paper that ends up in recycling bins at the office. And it can be made from other recycled fibers like cotton.

In choosing your invitations, environmental advocates recommend that you buy:

◎ Paper with the most recycled content, preferably 100 percent post-consumer waste (PCW) recycled paper.

◎ Chlorine-free paper or paper not bleached with chlorine or chlorine derivatives.

◎ Vegetable-based inks such as those made with soy oil.

Check out the Environmental Paper Network (www. EnvironmentalPaper.org) in North Carolina and Conservatree (www.conservatree.org) in San Francisco to learn more about paper and for more consumer tips. If for any reason you end up selecting paper from virgin fiber, at least look for the seal of approval of the Forest Stewardship Council (FSC) at www.fscus.org, which certifies that the paper came from logging that did not involve, as it often has, habitat destruction, water pollution, or the displacement of people and wildlife.

But Joshua Martin of the Environmental Paper Network notes: "There's really no need for virgin fiber. You can get beautiful paper that is recycled or made from byproducts. This adds extra value to your invitation, it shows people you care."

INVITATIONS: TREE-FREE, PLANTABLE, OR PAPERLESS

Who hasn't received an e-mail with an admonition at the bottom? "Please think before you print this e-mail." Some people (OK, I) may find such messages a tad preachy, but there is no question that a more judicious use of paper has caught on. Book publishers are also gradually switching from virgin fiber to recycled paper. Stewart, Tabori & Chang, my publisher, printed the book you are holding on recycled paper and used soy-based inks (for more information please see the copyright page).

Stationery companies have also stepped up to meet the demands of green consumers. You'll find plenty of selection in wedding invitations that are chlorine-free, which means that dioxins and chlorinated toxic pollutants are not being released into wastewater during the bleaching process; that are made of recycled materials; and that use vegetable-based inks rather that those with a petroleum base.

Some offerings are unexpectedly creative. Wedding invitations can be found in paper infused with garlic skins or coffee chaff. Some come with embedded seeds so that they can be planted in a pot and turned into sunflowers. Some are colored with vegetables and herbs and decorated with fern and pressed flowers.

For those unfamiliar with the aesthetics of ecologically sound paper, do what Margo and Ben did. They first visited a stationery store to hold and touch samples. "That made it much easier," says Margo. "We liked the feel of the paper—an old-fashioned, rustic (slightly bumpy) feel."

Margo and Ben chose simple, cream-colored invitations and RSVP cards made of reclaimed cotton handmade paper, which is made with remnants from the garment industry. They ordered from Oblation Papers & Press (www.OblationPapers.com), an Oregon company that sells at retail outlets and online. Ben personalized the invitation with his own illustration—most companies will let you design your own graphic, the couple say.

While recycled paper at one time cost more than conventional paper, prices have become competitive. One way to cut costs—by $1 to $2 per invitation sometimes—is to make the cards yourself. Kelly Nichols of Danville, California, bought a do-it-yourself kit from InviteSite.com with 100 percent recycled and tree-free orange (handmade) sheets and envelopes that Kelly complemented with red paper for a scarlet backdrop. And Kelly made the paper for the save-the-date cards herself with shredded junk mail. She shredded the mail, made the pulp, and pressed the paper, coloring it (with food coloring) yellow with tinges of orange. She then ran white sheets of 100 percent post consumer waste-recycled paper through the printer with the save-the-date information and glued that to the yellow, handmade paper. She stamped the cards with "Handmade paper made by Kelly & friends."

Kelly got her desired beautiful look, but she notes the do-it-yourself process may be too laborious for a harried couple in the middle of their wedding planning. "I thought, "I'll never do that again," she admits. Lucky for

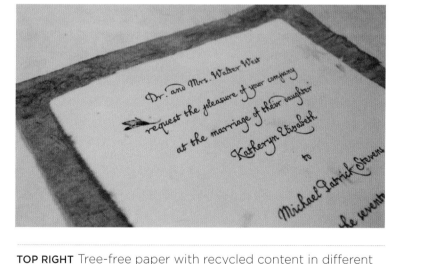

TOP RIGHT Tree-free paper with recycled content in different styles, including Periwinkle, Blue Garden, and Chocolate.
BOTTOM RIGHT Lotka paper, made in the highlands of Nepal from the bark of the Daphne bush, provides the background for this seeded invitation. (All products from Of The Earth.)

TOP LEFT Invitations made with paper that has been recycled, dyed with vegetables and embedded with seeds. **BOTTOM LEFT** Vegetable-dyed "Eco-Twist" recycled paper ribbon

you, there are many companies that can do the heavy lifting. Go online and you'll find a dizzying selection of green invitations.

To get an idea of the offerings, this is what one company, Of the Earth (www.CustomPaper.com) in Washington, lets you do, in whole or in parts:

◎ Start with 100 percent recycled paper or paper made with industrial cotton scraps.

◎ Add ingredients such as dried flowers, herbs, and vegetables to create your own handmade paper.

◎ Choose carrots or beets to color the paper, or wildflower and bachelor button seeds to give the paper new life as a sprout in a pot.

◎ Embellish the invitations with vegetable-dyed spools of hand-twisted recycled paper ribbons, pressed flower stickers, or fern attachments.

Of course, you can always skip paper altogether. Stephanie Hibbert and Mark Pearson went paperless for their fall 2007 wedding but gave their guests fair warning. The couple sent out save the date postcards and

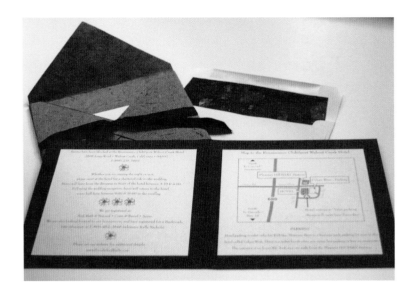

A do-it-yourself kit from InviteSite.com helps Kelly Nichols make her own recycled paper invitations.

e-mails to 150 guests directing them to their wedding website, where the invitation was posted. In the postcard they explained why (See "In Their Own Words" on page 87). "This is one of the things we got the most excited about," Stephanie says. "We would introduce our family and friends to a new way of sharing information and a low-impact way to communicate things about the wedding."

IN THEIR OWN WORDS:
HOW ONE COUPLE COMMUNICATED THEIR PAPERLESS APPROACH

Once they decided to go paperless for their wedding, Stephanie Hibbert and Mark Pearson still needed to find a way to communicate to their guests their green approach to invitations. Their idea: Use the save-the-date postcard to explain no more paper would be forthcoming and to give guests the address and log-in information for their wedding website.

But coming up with the right language took some effort. Mark, who hails from De Moines, Iowa, felt their first draft was a little too "hippy-dippy," too "out-there-California-freak," Stephanie says. So they compromised to appeal to both bikers from the Midwest and tofu eaters from the Bay Area. This is what they wrote:

It's a nice day for a . . . Green Wedding! It is our honor to invite you to experience and observe the amazing love we have for each other, the deep appreciation we have for you, and the profound respect we have for our natural environment and resources.

We believe in and understand our responsibility to minimize our impact on the earth, while providing an unforgettable experience for our friends, our family, and ourselves. Our intention is to minimize the "footprint" our wedding makes on the planet while embracing and enjoying the abundance in our lives, as well as nurturing our spirits.

We are thrilled to invite you to participate in sharing and gathering information about our event by engaging in a paperless process. Please visit our website and provide us with your e-mail address.

Make WeddingWebsites.com, which runs Tripadvisor-like comparisons among wedding websites, along with reviews by users, your first stop when shopping around for a site. Bradley Newton, a photographer and web designer who runs Wedding Websites from Dallas, Texas, says couples can get a perfectly good site for about $100.

When considering the many offerings, make sure you take advantage of the free trials to spot any potential problems. Glitches users complain about the most include:

◎ Poor customer service

◎ Slow uploads and connection speeds

◎ Links that don't work

◎ Trouble accessing the site or sites that disappear

Another tip: Make sure you keep copies of photos and "anything that's precious to you that you put in the website," Newton says.

Newton's five picks for well-run sites are:

◎ WeddingWindow.com

◎ WedShare.com

◎ MyEvent.com

◎ WedQuarters.com

◎ MyWedding.com (free)

Looking for a wedding website? Go to WeddingWebsites.com first to check what other couples are saying about the companies they used.

SAY IT WITH PAPER?

You can use the same green options for engagement announcements, shower invitations, thank-you notes, save the date cards, ceremony programs, escort cards, place cards, menu cards and guest books. But you may want to cut down on paper, period. How about writing names on pebbles or leaves in glitter instead of place cards or escort cards? Or having tables share fewer menu cards? And who needs a program anyway?

Go lighter on any kind of paper by choosing smaller invitations and avoiding additional envelopes, forgoing the traditional envelope-within-an-envelope style. Send postcard reply cards to avoid yet more envelopes.

KEEPING LOVED ONES IN THE LOOP: THE WEDDING WEBSITE

While the paper invitation and thank-you notes hold on for dear life, wedding websites are slowly replacing almost every other correspondence. There is no greener way than the electronic way (as long as you turn off the computer when it's not being used, of course), but wedding websites have many other advantages, including convenience, and audio and video capabilities. They also provide a creative platform for showcasing a couple's love story, from proposal to honeymoon.

Your guests' eyes will mist as they read about how you two met. They will get excited when you link them to pictures of the awesome venue. Post pictures and biographies of the bridal party, and everyone will know who's who way before the "I do's." List the schedule of wedding-related activities, and your guests will get a taste of the fun to come. In short, the wedding website can create buzz worthy of an Oscar campaign!

With a wedding website you can:

◎ Post the invitation, directions to the reception and ceremony, addresses and maps for accommodations, schedule of activities, and other information.

◎ Have guests RSVP, pick menu items, or e-mail you.

◎ Manage invites and RSVPs for separate guest lists for multiple wedding-related events, like the rehearsal dinner or after-wedding brunch. (With passwords for different visitors to access different pages.)

◎ Link to other websites for guests to go to your registry, book their hotel rooms, and check out the venue.

◎ Keep guests updated about last-minute changes.

◎ Offer a recap of the celebration, and honeymoon, with photos and video.

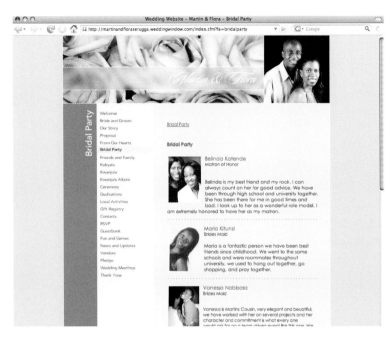

A wedding website plays a key role in the wedding planning of Flora Kiggundu and Martin Serugga in Uganda, enabling the couple to share preparations with friends and relatives who, according to local custom, help defray the costs of the celebration.

If you are sold on the idea of a wedding website, search online for "wedding websites" to find dozens of ready-made sites that allow customization. It is recommended that you get the site up at least six months before the wedding so that guests have plenty of time to get acquainted with it.

Some websites offer more than others, and there's a wide range in price, from free to those that will run you several hundred dollars for a hosting period of at least a year (see "The Cyberjungle" on page 88). But, as always, be mindful of the guests who won't go near a computer. One solution: Plan on a limited use of paper invitations, RSVP cards, and other inserts for guests you think will prefer the traditional.

Flora Kiggundu, 28, and Martin Serugga, 33, signed up with WeddingWindow.com. for their June 2008 nuptials. Flora and Martin, who have a young son, Israel Luke, and co-own an investment company involved in media, real estate, and commercial forestry, live in Kampala, Uganda. I thought their story was so charming and instructive that my American readers could benefit from it.

Imagine having no choice but to invite two hundred guests, including extended family, friends, and associates, to your wedding because of cultural norms. Imagine all these guests having a say in the preparations because they all help pay for your wedding. This is what Flora and Martin faced.

"People want to be consulted for their views because here the wedding costs are met with the financial and moral support of the couple's friends and relatives," Martin explained in an e-mail. "The traditional way of including others in any wedding preparations is what we call 'wedding meetings.' This is where one invites people, say once a week, to discuss and make contributions to the preparations and wedding budget."

In their case, the wedding website took the place of the traditional weekly meetings, and it kicked off the preparations earlier than the usual two months prior to the wedding. The website was conceived in January 2008, and by the end of February, it had had more than 500 hits.

"We were able to raise more than 10 percent of our wedding budget through pledges in a few weeks," Martin said. "The results were simply amazing." There was one other benefit: Typically, a Ugandan couple would have to drive long distances to personally announce their wedding plans to certain relatives in person. "In our culture it is considered disrespectful to inform, particularly elders, about your wedding by phone," Martin noted. But, surprisingly, these same relatives welcomed the website, he said, so the couple were able to avoid the trips and the carbon emissions they would have produced.

"We are very active in planting trees in our community, and keeping the environment green is high on our agenda," Martin said. "We are happy to say that, through the website, a small contribution has been made."

CHAPTER 6

THE DÉCOR
NATIVES OR JET-SETTERS?

At one point, Katie Malouf considered plain old grass. Yes, simple blades of grass. In this case, in a vase. For her wedding. Anything, she insisted, but flowers. Katie was wrestling with a challenge for environmentally conscious brides: How do you manage a responsible wedding with these essential but problematic beauties?

A Washington, D.C.–based advocate on economic justice campaigns for Oxfam International, the global relief organization, Katie, 27, had once visited a flower farm in Colombia and it made an impression. She met a woman in her twenties who was organizing the workers, most of them young women, to demand living wages, job security, and safe use of pesticides.

Even more than food crops, flowers require perfection. We can forgive an oddly shaped or blemished tomato, but a rose? "We don't want flowers with little bites taken out of leaves where bugs had their lunch," notes Amy Stewart, author of *Flower Confidential: The Good, the Bad and the Beautiful in the Business of Flowers* (Algonquin Books, 2007). To ensure those spotless petals and flawless shapes, growers often resort to the heavy use of herbicides, fungicides, and insecticides that ward off bugs and disease. While great for aesthetics, toxic

Veriflora-certified tulips, roses, peonies and ranunculus try to steal the show at the wedding of Katie Malouf and Joe Bous at the Orange County Museum of Art in California.

chemicals can end up in the local water supplies, affecting both wildlife and humans; in some instances unprotected workers have suffered illnesses when exposed to these chemicals. A study from the University of Southern Denmark released in 2008 found that female workers who became pregnant while working in greenhouses for cut flowers and potted plants had an increased risk of giving birth to boys with abnormal reproductive organs. The researchers found that the problems occurred despite safeguards like gloves and other protective equipment.

So for couples bent on a green celebration, the questions "How was it grown?" and "Where does it come from?" are especially relevant. Some may decide to do without the bouquets and decorations because of the labor issues and the limited reuse value of cut flowers.

TOP LEFT A bride's bouquet features Veriflora-certified Vendela roses. **BOTTOM LEFT** Certified Esperance roses in a wood box hang on a ribbon.

TOP RIGHT Bridesmaids' bouquets are kept in water in a Blumebox, a container made of recycled paper. **BOTTOM RIGHT** A certified Vendela rose brightens the place setting.(All arrangements by Christine Saunders of The Spiraled Stem)

But flowers add such elegance, color, and élan to a wedding, not to mention emotion, that many brides would feel cheated without them.

"I know brides who want flowers from their mother's bouquet or that they remember from their grandmother's garden," Stewart says. Luckily, the flower industry, which provides a livelihood to tens of thousands of workers in poor countries, is becoming greener, as Katie soon discovered.

Nearly 80 percent of the cut flowers we buy in the United States come from other countries—most are from Colombia but many are also imported from Ecuador, the Netherlands, Costa Rica, Canada, and Mexico, according to the Society of American Florists. When Katie saw flower production first-hand in Colombia, she had been distraught. "If they got pregnant or sick, they were fired," she says of the workers she met. "The list goes on and on. I felt like, Urgh! I don't want to buy flowers anymore." When the time came to plan her May 2008 wedding to her boyfriend of five years, Joe Bous, 35, the owner of a computer software consulting business, Katie's initial attitude was A.B.F—anything but flowers. She began looking into simpler potted plants or vases with all grass or all bamboo for décor. Then she came across a flower designer in California, Christine Saunders, who suggested another option: Veriflora-certified flowers, which come with a guarantee that they have not been dunked in chemicals or grown under abusive working conditions.

The Veriflora stamp of approval is one among several eco-labels that have sprung up to vouch for better flower-growing methods, imposing strict environmental and labor standards on growers, including minimizing or phasing out pesticide use. Another label, "USDA Organic," which is regulated by the United States Department of Agriculture, bans the use of any synthetic pesticides and fertilizers altogether. A third common label, "Fair Trade Certified," is similar to Veriflora but also pays a premium to farmers so they will invest in community programs like day care centers. Leading American flower growers, distributors, and retailers supported the creation of sustainable standards for flowers sold in the United States starting in the early 2000s, following the model of European environmental and labor groups, which had already come up with labeling programs in their own countries.

Whether you object to chemically treated flowers and demand organic or you're concerned about the treatment of farm workers, these labels are essential for one key reason: They let you know exactly what you're buying. Katie liked what the Veriflora label represented. Forget the grass. "When flowers are in a room, the room is 100 percent prettier," she says. "It's one of the most beautiful things in nature. How can you have a wedding without flowers?"

Well, some couples can. Beautiful as they can be, flowers can eat up 10 percent of the wedding budget, so it is not difficult for eco-conscious couples to begin wondering whether the blooms are worth all that money. They are perishable, aren't they? Where is the reuse value? And most are flown in from halfway across the globe, so what about all those carbon emissions produced in the shipping?

At the other end of the spectrum, of course, stand those who buy their blooms for their perfume or pretty colors, unaware of any horror stories about toxic chemicals or dangerous working conditions. After all, flowers are not food. "People think, Oh, it doesn't matter. I'm not going to eat the flowers," notes Katie. And flowers grown with toxic pesticides have not been found to pose a health danger to consumers, so what's the big deal?

Florists report they are asked all the time: "Aren't all flowers organic?" Wherever you stand on these important questions, you should know a few basics about flowers to make an informed choice.

WHY CARE ABOUT FLOWERS

The public, so keen on scrutinizing food, lagged about fifteen years before questioning the green credentials of flowers, since flowers are luxury items and are not eaten, says the Organic Trade Association. But the environmentally correct flower is very much on the consumer green agenda now, alongside produce, cars, and homes.

In Colombia and Ecuador, countries with mild climates ideal for flower production, only a small minority of farms had adopted occupational health measures or safer farming methods by the first decade of the twenty-first century, according to watchdog groups like the International Labor Rights Forum in Washington, D.C. The problems at flower farms in South America, the groups say, have included pesticides so toxic they are illegal in the United States, poverty-level wages, and child labor.

In the United States, flower production is smaller and more regulated, but the industry has still had to do some cleaning up. For example, officials with Veriflora say, they have found evidence that workers and supervisors at some farms are not adequately trained.

"Workers are sometimes asked to enter greenhouses or fields before the proper amount of time has elapsed since a chemical application was made," says Linda Brown, executive vice president of Scientific Certification Systems, which certifies farms that meet the label's standards. "By educating growers and establishing written policies regarding chemical usage, we have been able to document changes that ensure that reentry times are being properly respected."

A few weeks before Valentine's Day 2008, I visited the largest domestic rose grower, California Pajarosa Floral in Watsonville, California. California Pajarosa, which grows ten million roses a year hydroponically in 17 acres of greenhouses, had long limited its pesticide use by relying on predatory mites. Still, the farm had to invest about

FLOWER-LESS: ALTERNATIVES TO FLOWERS

If you find the idea of cut flowers wasteful, there are ways you can decorate without them. Just avoid alternatives that may not be that much better.

For example, some couples consider dried flowers because they can be reused, but what's the point, asks Christine Saunders, a green wedding flower designer. "A dried flower was at one point a live flower," she notes. Potted plants are also an option, but are you sure they weren't coated in pesticides?

Avoid these pitfalls by looking for:

◎ Certified potted flowers and plants that can be replanted.

◎ A venue in a natural setting, like a park or botanical garden, where the flowers will be just another guest.

◎ Paper flowers. For a wedding with 140 guests, says Corina Beczner, the events planner in San Francisco, the couple chose big, hanging paper balls and paper flower centerpieces. The bride got the guests involved by having a dozen female relatives and girlfriends over for a flower-making afternoon tea party. "It was the bride's 'bridal shower' of sorts," says Beczner. "They all sat around the garden in the sun and made the flowers after eating and enjoying some time together."

◎ Corsages made of scraps of fabrics for the mothers of the groom and bride. Elisa Jimenez, of *Project Runway*, is one fashion designer who makes them.

◎ Edible centerpieces such as bowls filled with colorful fruit and vegetables or baskets of bread.

$100,000 in improvements to comply with all the regulations required to earn the Veriflora certification, such as planting trees around the farm to control erosion and recycling water both for conservation and to reuse some of the fertilizer runoff.

That can be expensive, but Paul Furman, the farm's manager, noted that cost is not the only roadblock standing in the way of better environmental practices. Even committed producers like California Pajarosa, he said, can't totally eliminate pesticides unless better science comes along. Predatory mites do not work 100 percent of the time. Large commercial growers need to worry about yield and quality first, he said, because "if we don't have sellable flowers, we can't be in business."

Growers, however, can still take more earth-friendly measures, such as spot-treating plants in trouble rather than spraying the whole crop with pesticides. Peter J. Moran, executive vice president and CEO of the Society of American Florists, whose members include retailers and growers in the United States and overseas, says even growers not certified by any labeling program have been "trying to make sure to get as much yield as they can, using the best practices they can."

The headwreath of a flower girl features Veriflora-certified light pink and ivory spray roses.

As with many green products, deciding about flowers can leave you scratching your head. Flowers from Ecuador, for instance, require no energy-intensive climate controls because of the ideal growing conditions, but they do need to be shipped long distances. Flowers from a local farm will not travel as far, but may have consumed a large amount of energy if they need to grow in a heated greenhouse.

When looking at the certified flower options, consider local and seasonal flowers first to cut down on transportation and heating emissions. Most United States flower production, more than 70 percent, is centered in California. But Washington, Florida, Hawaii, Oregon, and New Jersey have a significant commercial flower business, too, so if you're lucky to live in those states it may be easy to go with flowers that are blooming near you at the time of the wedding. Look for certified organic or sustainably grown products like those carrying the Veriflora label. Try LocalHarvest.org, which lists who grows what and where and allows you to search for farms and farmers' markets by zip code. (A farm may not be certified because of the cost and technical criteria involved in winning certification, but it may still use organic methods. Question the farmer to find out.)

You could set your wedding date by flower season, but the reality is that the flower market is dominated by imports. If you hold out for local flowers, you may end up with a very limited selection. If local is not an option—if, say, you're getting married in Minnesota in the middle

Having first beautified the aisle for the ceremony, these gerbera daisies later double as a centerpiece.

of winter—go with certified imports, which get the nod from major environmental groups such as the Natural Resources Defense Council.

"The whole idea behind green weddings is about what kind of impact are we making on the planet overall," Stewart notes, referring to other flower-growing countries. "I care about the woman who cut my flowers. She's also somebody's bride."

Wedding floral designers like Christine Saunders, owner of The Spiraled Stem (www.TheSpiraledStem.com) in Anaheim, California, says she preferred the Veriflora label over USDA Organic or Fair Trade Certified because it focused on both the environment and the workers and

offered most of the flowers brides like: hydrangeas, vendela roses (which are ivory), tulips, and calla lilies.

Couples can also go to online suppliers such as OrganicBouquet.com and OrganicStyle.com (both retail) and EcoFlowers.com (wholesale), all of them run by Gerald Prolman, a pioneer in introducing sustainable flowers to the American market in 2001. A bride anywhere can ask her local florist to order her chosen blooms from EcoFlowers.com, which carries certified sustainably grown flowers from the United States, Ecuador, and Colombia, and then have the florist design the arrangements and transport them to the venue.

LEFT Reusable vases help dress up the reception table.
RIGHT Bridesmaids' bouquets make a second appearance as decorations in mason jars.

Flowers grown with sustainable practices look indistinguishable from conventionally grown flowers, florists say. Quality is largely dictated by the handling and whether the flowers were kept chilled from farm to retail store.

Also, vase life and fragrance have more to do with the variety of flower and its breeding. Most roses are bred to be long-lasting rather than fragrant because perfumed roses open faster and are more vulnerable to pests.

Flower type also determines price. Saunders notes that calla lilies or peonies will cost you more than gerbera daisies. Availability is another important variable. Cost goes up during high-demand seasons like May and June, which includes Mother's Day and graduations galore. The time around Valentine's Day is another season to avoid if you want to save money. And don't forget how the cost of labor can affect flower prices. At the flower shop, roses need to be stripped of thorns and bad petals, Saunders says, while a gerbera daisy requires little handling.

Her budget tips:

◎ Choose large flowers so you'll need fewer of them for the centerpieces or arrangements.

◎ A short centerpiece is more economical than a tiered one with the extra cost of a larger container and more flowers.

◎ A one-variety theme is easier than arranging multiple varieties and therefore tends to cost less.

Stewart says some retailers deal in high-end organic and sustainable flowers that cost more because of their higher quality. An esperance rose, for example, has an enormous head and is bred to retain a lush open shape for weeks. "It's like champagne," Stewart says of the differences in quality and prices.

Katie Malouf says it was a pleasant surprise that her sustainable choices were no more expensive than conventional ones (although that may change as the certified brands become more popular). "It's one of those rare times when you are not forced to choose between doing the right thing and your checkbook," she says.

SAY CHEESE:
DIGITAL PHOTOGRAPHY AND VIDEOGRAPHY

Given all the stresses of planning a wedding, it is good to know that going green in your photography can actually make things easier. Most wedding photographers shoot with digital cameras (as opposed to film), which save on paper and processing chemicals. You don't need negatives or printed proofs. You can share pictures with your guests by uploading images to a webpage and printing just the ones you want for your photo album (consider vintage leather).

"If they are having photographers print up photos for them, they should insist that all prints should be archival pigment prints printed on 100 percent cotton paper (as opposed to resin-coated papers)," says Joe Zammit-Lucia, a photographer who authored a report on green photo paper in collaboration with the Nature Conservancy

("Green-in-Print" at www. J2LImages.com.) "Not only is this the most environmentally friendly approach but it also produces the longest lasting prints without fading."

Today you can even find photographers who offset their travel, billing themselves as "carbon-neutral." And you can have

friends and relatives capture candid moments throughout the wedding by renting cameras and video equipment instead of resorting to disposable cameras.

"It's a great way to reduce waste and is a lot more fun and functional than disposables," says Jonathan Bailor, owner of CameraRenter.com, an online

camera rental service based in Washington. "Disposable cameras take bad pictures and, since they are disposables, sit unused or are used to take three pictures of the floor."

With digital videography, there's not much to worry about except the added cost. Videography is as expensive as photography, so you need double the budget to document your nuptials. A survey commissioned by the Wedding and Event Videographers Association International, a trade group known as WEVA (www.WEVA.com), showed 60 percent of brides who didn't have their weddings videotaped wish they had. Self-serving, no doubt, but the survey rang true to me.

When I got married, we wanted to save money, so my fiancé and I did without the video camera. It seemed excessive. But whenever I look at our wedding pictures, which I thoroughly enjoy, I wonder what it would be like to see the same scenes—my mother dancing with my father-in-law, my gorgeous groom making a toast in broken Spanish—in action. Looking back, long after the plates have been cleared and the flowers have composted, I feel like a fool for scrimping on something as lasting as a video.

So that you don't end up with regrets like mine, have your video, but don't go crazy. You don't need a $10,000 Hollywood production, just video footage you will treasure.

You can green your flowers even more if you reuse. A way to maximize the use of flowers is to arrange to have them taken to a hospital or a nursing home after the wedding. Regarding shipping, you can patronize vendors like OrganicBouquet.com, which offsets emissions by buying carbon credits.

Are you feeling better about having flowers at your wedding? Some party planners have turned to potted plants as an alternative (Veriflora certifies those, too), but advocates of keeping tradition alive argue there's no need to compromise on flowers in order to be green.

Katie's wedding, attended by 125 guests at the Orange County Museum of Art, featured tulips as the starring bloom in tiered vertical arrangements with cut oranges, in centerpieces surrounded by pink roses and in the bouquets. I asked Katie why tulips, and she told me, "They're kind of whimsical. The way the stems bend. They change colors."

But there was one more reason, closer to her heart: "They've always been my mother's favorite flower."

LEFT A centerpiece of sustainable orange tulips and coral roses in a short, square glass vase. **RIGHT** Rose petals decorate the wedding cake. (Flowers by Christine Saunders of the Spiraled Stem.)

With Oscar parties, museum galas, and many other upscale celebrations jumping on the sustainable bandwagon, it was no surprise that Girari, an event furnishings company in Beverly Hills whose high-end minimalist furniture is made of recycled metal, sponsored such a thing as the "Wedding Reception Table Decorating Shootout." The contest, which I attended in Los Angeles in early 2008, drew contestants like Joe Moller, whose centerpiece used a large glass terrarium filled with recycled broken glass colored red and black using eco-friendly paints. The glass served as soil to secure 36-inch tall dogwood branches and cherry blossom branches. On the surface of the glass table he had painted "tablescapes" of Japanese tattoos and fish with water soluble paint.

"Unless the clients are themselves already eco-friendly, chances are their perception of green elements conjure up images of big blue trash cans or brownish napkins made from recycled materials," Moller says of the misperceptions among some clients. "Elements like centerpieces made from all reclaimed hardware can look better than traditional elements made from plastic."

But you don't have to be a professional to let your creativity infuse the décor at your wedding. Two weeks before her wedding in Austin's Zilker Metropolitan Park, Karin Ascot rummaged through her neighbors' recycling bins early one morning (to beat the collection truck), looking for glass bottles. Her bounty included bottles for vinegar, olive oil, and spirits in all kinds of shapes and colors. She removed the labels and filled each bottle with two roses and a sprig of rosemary from her neighborhood gardens. Set on the park's picnic tables, surrounded by tea light candles, the bottles made splendid centerpieces.

"It was just pretty," Karin says. "People said they really liked them. I gave away a bunch of them at the end of the evening."

The sky is the limit for a bride's ideas for decorations, so here are a few more to get you going:

◎ Consider tables a blank canvas. Moller (www. JoeMoller.com) also uses Legos, board game markers, and other children's toys to decorate them. Why not write the wedding menu on the table with water soluble paint and do without menu cards, Moller suggests.

◎ Moller suggests getting vintage ribbons at the flea market to tie them around the stems of glasses.

◎ Another "shootout" contestant, Fresh Events Company, used champagne flutes as elegant decoration by filling them with white biodegradable confetti.

◎ Why not have guests eat the centerpieces? Edibles include bowls with apples, grapes, oranges, and other colorful fruit; tomatoes and other veggies; baskets of breads; and bouquets of lollipops with multicolored wrappers. Try mixing up centerpieces table to table.

◎ Feature potted plants and flowers that can continue their lives at a guest's home. Floral designer Christine Saunders suggests decorating potted plants with a few fresh flowers in the colors of the wedding

A birch bark centerpiece holds a nest filled with buckeye nuts.

to enhance the overall look and feel. For containers, she recommends rented vases in styles that avoid the use of foam or "blumeboxes," which are made with 100 percent recycled post-consumer waste paper.

◎ Candlelight is romantic and saves on electricity use. A word on candles: the Consumer Product Safety Commission has banned the sale of lead-wick candles, so lead emissions from candles are no longer a concern. Many green websites recommend vegetable-based soy and beeswax candles as a healthier alternative to petroleum-based paraffin wax candles, but there is no conclusive scientific evidence linking type of candle to specific hazardous effects. Norman Edelman, the American Lung Association's Chief Medical Officer, says vegetable-based candles are more eco-friendly because they come from renewable sources, but that candle smoke does not pose toxicity issues except as a possible irritant to people with respiratory problems like asthma.

◎ Find quilts and vintage tablecloths. Danielle Venokur, of dvGreen in New York, says you get the reuse value when you go to rental companies for linens, but she notes that the companies have been slow to embrace eco-fabrics. She finds basic organic cotton easily but "the texture tends to be a little more casual than elegant." For a high-end wedding, having the tablecloths custom-made with organic materials and nontoxic dyes is prohibitive for most brides, so she suggests looking for vintage fabrics for a more affordable upscale look.

◎ For her wedding, Ali Wood of Brooklyn, New York, put together her tableware from thrift shops and by collecting pieces from relatives.

CHAPTER 7

THE GUESTS
BRING OUT THE (CARBON) CALCULATOR!

Ah, the wonders of a September wedding: a palette of brilliant earth tones, images of baked squash, and, of course, sipping Champagne under the golden fall leaves. But when Elizabeth Levy, 29, and Ryan Bouldin, 27, of Boston, began planning their autumn nuptials in a meadow in the Berkshires, something decidedly unromantic made it to the top of their to-do list—"carbon offsets."

Carbon dioxide emissions are hardly the stuff of romance, but given what scientists have taught us about the dangerous role of greenhouse gases in climate change, carbon offsets are becoming as common as the organic menu at green weddings. As Elizabeth, an environmental research analyst, and Ryan, a chemical engineering student, dealt with caterers, arranged for hotel accommodations, and sent out invitations to 125 guests, they also assumed responsibility for estimating the carbon dioxide (CO2) their guests would spew into the atmosphere while driving or flying to their wedding in 2007. This was no back-of-the-envelope exercise: They had to figure out the miles each guest would travel, their mode of transportation, and then bring out the carbon calculator.

How important was this? "I feel we're being a bit consumptive by having a big wedding," Elizabeth said a few months into her wedding planning. "This is kind of to atone. We want to make sure the guests know that the environment is pretty important to us, too."

Elizabeth Levy and Ryan Bouldin and the school bus they used to take their guests to the wedding.

OFFSETTING THE GLOBAL WARMING IMPACT OF THE CELEBRATION

The emissions and refuse produced by the wedding itself—in energy use, in waste headed for landfills—are often slight, particularly if you have chosen a green venue, compared to the guests' long-distance travel. Think of messy elephants leaving a big, ugly footprint on the white carpet called Earth. Guests are not exactly elephants, but big parties can be, metaphorically speaking, and some couples feel it is only right to clean up after their festivities.

As we green our lives, buying carbon offsets or credits from both nonprofits and for-profit companies has emerged as a popular, though somewhat controversial, way to fight some of the negative consequences of modern amenities. The companies funnel the money you pay for your travel emissions, or those from lifestyle activities, to green projects such as replacing power from coal-fired generating plants with renewable energy sources like windmills.

Companies like Terrapass, Carbonfund, and Native Energy have proliferated to help the carbon-conscious become, in effect, carbon-neutral. Consumers, from air carriers to sofa makers—even to touring bands like the Rolling Stones—have responded in droves, spending

tens of millions of dollars on these offsets. In Southern California, where I live, it is not unusual to spot bumper stickers such as "This car's CO2 balanced by Terrapass."

Of course, a more direct way of reducing damage to the environment is by adjusting your behavior. Buy a hybrid car or ride mass transit. Set the thermostat at home down a few degrees in the winter. Certainly, no amount of personal investing to neutralize CO2 emissions should replace steps to reduce your personal impact. The average American, research shows, is responsible for about 20 tons of CO2 emissions a year, which is double what the average European or Japanese produces.

None other than Mr. Green himself, former Vice President Al Gore, came under attack because of his huge personal consumption of electricity—191,000 kilowatt hours a year, which translates to a $1,200 monthly utility bill, at his 10,000-square-foot home in Nashville, Tennessee. Gore said he compensated for his energy use by buying carbon offsets but, during Congressional testimony on global warming in early 2007, one Republican Senator needled him by calling offsets gimmicks for the wealthy. (Mr. Gore later installed solar panels and geothermal heating to make his home less of an energy hog.)

In other words, offsets, while potentially useful, are not a waiver. If you're buying carbon offsets only to relieve the guilt of driving an SUV, you may be sabotaging your own conservation efforts. "Carbon offsetting is kind of the last resort strategy," says Anja Kollmuss,

TOP LEFT Place cards printed on 100 percent recycled paper hang from a garden trellis. **TOP RIGHT** Ryan and Elizabeth. **BOTTOM LEFT** Local, seasonal, and organic flowers decorate the tables at the reception. **BOTTOM RIGHT** A local and organic display for the cocktail hour.

an associate scientist with the Stockholm Environment Institute, an independent research affiliate of Tufts University. "The first strategy would be to avoid the emissions or reduce them."

Some marrying couples try to steer guests to mass transit. For their public transit–themed wedding in an old trolley barn in October 2006, Anna and Matt Cherry, of Atlanta, attached to their invitations directions to the wedding via MARTA, Atlanta's rapid transit rail and bus

Anna and Matt Cherry at "The Gulch" in downtown Atlanta, the site where railroad lines used to converge more than 100 years ago.

system. Anna, 26, a community organizer for the Sierra Club, and Matt, 29, an urban planner, had met working on a project to convert old, unused rails into a new transit line. "For Matt and me this was just such a big part of our life, and we wanted to share it with our family and friends," the bride says. "At least half of the people took MARTA. There were not a ton of cars parked outside."

During the ceremony, the pastor worked the public transportation theme into his comments, talking about Atlanta's traffic problems and about how Matt and Anna were helping promote sustainable modes of transportation. After the reception, the couple had their two hundred guests follow them three buildings down to a MARTA station so they could board a train—he still in his tuxedo, she in full white gown—to travel five stops to their hotel downtown.

As they stood on the platform, guests waved and cheered from a balcony. And once the couple entered the train, passengers joined in the revelry. "We got on the train and people were clapping," says Anna, who remembers the commotion as one of the highlights of her big day. "Everybody was saying 'Congratulations!' and asking, 'Where are you going on your honeymoon?'"

The answer: A trip to the Pacific Northwest involving travel by train, light rail, streetcar, ferry, kayak and bicycle. "The only car we were in was a hybrid taxi in Vancouver," Anna says.

THE RIDES: WAYS TO KEEP CARBON EMISSIONS DOWN

Couples can do more than purchase carbon offsets when trying to make their wedding-related transportation environmentally sound. Picking the right location for the wedding and good planning will make the difference between cleaner and more polluted air, and between a grumpy and a ready-to-party guest. Among the musts:

◎ Pick the venue that is closest to most guests to cut down on long-distance travel.

◎ Coordinate flying schedules so that guests arrive at around the same time to limit the number of pick-ups at the airport and to facilitate car rental sharing (preferably hybrid cars).

◎ Charter buses for groups of guests coming from the same city, say from New York to a wedding in Boston.

◎ Provide shuttle buses to transport guests from their hotel to the venue. Go the extra mile by looking for hybrid shuttle buses or those that run on bio-diesel fuel, which is derived from vegetable matter and has lower emissions than petroleum.

◎ Include directions to the wedding by subway, bus, and other mass transit on your wedding website or along with the invitation.

◎ Do you really need the limo? If you do, look into a hybrid as well.

HOW CARBON OFFSETS WORK

For emissions you can't avoid, such as those produced by family and friends attending your wedding, carbon offset companies offer to help undo the damage in tit-for-tat fashion: If you produce 6 tons worth of emissions, for example, you can help pay for a project that will absorb the 6 tons, like planting trees, or a project that would prevent another 6 tons from entering the atmosphere, like developing renewable sources of electricity.

Transportation is one of the worst sources of CO_2 emissions. Almost a third of the carbon dioxide produced in the United States comes from vehicles and airplanes, says the Environmental Protection Agency. But with some planning, travel emissions are among the easiest to offset. Online travel agencies like Expedia offer passengers a way to offset the flights booked through their websites. Major airlines offer voluntary carbon-offset programs, allowing passengers to calculate and pay carbon-offset fees when they buy their tickets. Car rental companies also offer offsets.

But brides like Elizabeth are also leading the way. That's when the carbon calculator comes in handy. The companies that sell carbon offsets provide travel calculators on their websites that allow users to plug in the departure cities and destinations to find the miles traveled and the volume of CO_2 emissions produced. The calculator then figures out how much it would cost to offset that flight per passenger. The total cost will depend on how far your guests are traveling and how much the company you use charges per ton of emissions. A single

roundtrip journey from California to New York produces about two tons of CO_2 emissions—the same as if you had

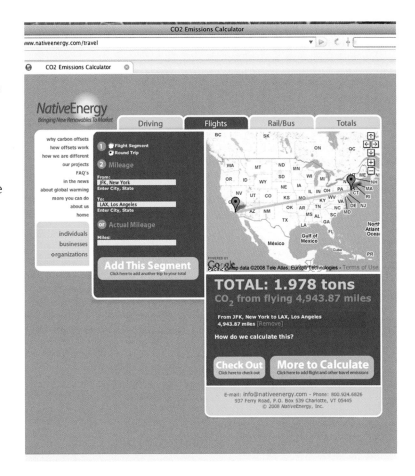

Native Energy's carbon offset calculator helps couples figure out the travel emissions produced by their wedding guests.

THE MARKETPLACE: CARBON OFFSET COMPANIES

So you want to offset your honeymoon trip to the Bahamas or your cousin's travel to your wedding from London? Dozens of companies sell carbon offsets, charging $5 to $20 per ton of CO_2 emissions. Some companies allow users to list their preferences so that their purchase goes to a specific project. Purchases from not-for-profit companies are tax deductible.

Some good ones are:

1. MyClimate.org, run by the nonprofit The Climate Protection Partnership, based in Switzerland.

2. Atmosfair.de, run by a German nonprofit focused on offsetting air travel.

3. NativeEnergy.com, a for-profit company majority-owned by the Intertribal Council on Utility Policy.

4. ClimateFriendly.com, run by a for-profit company in Australia.

In addition, try Travel Analytics at http://carbon.trx.com/Home. asp and The Environmental Protection Agency's epa.gov/climatechange/emissions/ind_calculator.html for help calculating your emissions for air travel and other activities.

A WORD OF CAUTION:
MAKING SURE YOUR MONEY IS FUNDING THE RIGHT PROJECTS

Some watchdog groups note that sometimes the money from carbon offset purchases go to projects that would have happened anyway. Sometimes it is also difficult for consumers to know whether their money is going to the right place or is doing any good.

The Stockholm Environment Institute (www.sei-us.org), a research affiliate of Tufts University, and the Tufts Climate Initiative (www.tufts.edu/tie/tci), recommend:

1. Looking for companies that use third-party verification to ensure the quality of carbon offsets. Look for the Gold Standard, the strictest available benchmark.

2. Checking whether your air travel emissions are calculated correctly by using this rule of thumb: A round-trip cross-country journey in the United States produces about 2 to 3 tons of CO_2 emissions per passenger; roundtrip from the East Coast to Europe produces about 3 to 4 tons. If the company's calculator comes up with much different numbers, it may not be giving you an accurate estimate of your emissions.

3. Looking carefully at the company's website to see that it lists its green projects in detail and gives you a good sense for how your money will be used. For high impact, donate your money to projects that help transition away from fossil fuels, such as building windmills or installing solar water heaters.

driven your car 4,000 miles, says Billy Connelly, a spokesman for Native Energy Inc., a carbon offset company that invests in environmental projects in Native American communities.

"Two tons is the same as the emissions generated by a room air conditioner for a full year, the average refrigerator for 8 months, or powering a laptop for just under 3 years," he says. Mitigating the impact of this plane ride would cost $24 in offsets with NativeEnergy.

THE CARBON OFFSET CALCULATOR

Most of Elizabeth and Ryan's 125 guests were from the Northeast, but many of Ryan's family members would be coming to the wedding from Indiana. Other friends would travel from California and, in the case of at least one guest, Elizabeth's sister, a Peace Corps worker, from Malawi, Africa. About fifty guests in all planned to fly in.

So, for example, if cousin Amber would be flying from Los Angeles to Albany and back, Native Energy says the 4,910 miles traveled would produce two tons of carbon dioxide emissions at a cost of $24 in offsets. Similarly, if cousin Julie were driving to the Berkshires from Indianapolis with her husband and two kids for the wedding, the 791 miles traveled in a medium-sized car would yield less than one ton of emissions at a cost of $12.

Elizabeth went with Terrapass, which has a calculator just for weddings at www.terrapass.com/wedding/weddingcalc.php. The total carbon footprint for her wedding came up to 105,000 pounds of CO_2 emissions at a cost of $555.

If you want the details, Elizabeth is happy to give them. Let's break it down into steps.

STEP 1: Terrapass's "Wedding Carbon Footprint Calculator" asks for the number of guests taking "short" (less than 2 hours), "medium" (about 4 hours), and "long" (longer than 4 hours) flights. Another way to look at it, Terrapass officials say, is to consider anything under 300 miles "short," anything more than 900 miles "long," and anything in between (300 to 900 miles) "medium." "I Google-mapped the distance that each person was flying," Elizabeth says. She came up with the following totals:

◎ 17 short flights

◎ 21 medium flights

◎ 15 long flights

STEP 2: The calculator then asked for the number of cars being driven to the wedding and the average one-way trip in miles. Elizabeth took the liberty here of adding more miles to account for other wedding-related driving, such as the 50-mile trip many guests would make from the airport to their hotel. "I guessed who was carpooling from home and included the 50 miles the people who were flying would be driving from the airport to their hotels," she says. "I guess it didn't capture the distance from the hotels to the wedding, but since we're having a bus to shuttle guests from the hotel to the venue, I guess that should cut down on trips, so I'm not too worried about that." Her estimates gave her 41 cars logging 202 miles on average.

STEP 3: The calculator then asks for hotel room nights, to offset the energy used in lodging guests. Her total: 100 hotel nights.

Newlyweds Anna and Matt Cherry get ready to board the train to travel back to their hotel.

Elizabeth plugged in all the required data and voila!—105,000 lbs of CO2 emissions, worth $555 in offsets. "The whole process was pretty easy, actually," Elizabeth says. "The most time-consuming part was getting the distances that people are driving and flying."

The hardest work may have been over—it took about an hour to calculate the offsets (I tried it)—but Elizabeth and Ryan had to decide one sticky issue: whether to pay for the offsets themselves or ask guests to put up the money. Some couples say they suggest carbon offsets to guests as a way of introducing them to a concept they may not be familiar with. "Be Green! Please carpool and/or offset the environmental impact of your travel at www.NativeEnergy.com," Joshua Houdek and Kristi Papenfuss, of Minneapolis, MN, wrote on the outside of the invitation along with directions to the ceremony and reception.

"A lot of our guests didn't have prior knowledge of carbon offsetting," says Kristi. "We asked for their participation if they felt they wanted to do something."

(Why Native Energy? The couple found the website easy to navigate, particularly for calculating individual trips. They also liked the projects the company funds.)

Elizabeth and Ryan opted for paying for the offsets themselves (which is also the preference of experts on wedding etiquette; see Chapter 3: The Gift Registry).

"I don't think it's fair to put that burden on the guests when this may not be something they care about," Elizabeth noted. But more and more people are beginning to care.

Some carbon offset vendors say more than 80 percent of their demand comes from individuals, most of whom want to offset their home energy use and their driving. But travel and events are also becoming a big part of the demand from offset customers.

Companies like Terrapass cater to green weddings with products like fancy certificates for display at the reception—proclaiming the event a "carbon balanced wedding" with a frame "handmade from salvaged Douglas fir." Connelly, the Native Energy spokesman, says his company has partnered up with Portovert, an online magazine for eco-conscious brides and grooms, to link information about offsets for weddings.

"I don't know any Native Energy clients who are buying carbon offsets because they want to assuage their guilt and go pollute some more," Connelly says. "People are doing this as part of an overall move toward sustainability. It's people who are already doing something to reduce their carbon imprint that are buying carbon offsets. All the folks that we talk to say they're selling their cars and buying a hybrid, they're shopping locally, they're buying organic hemp clothing."

Elizabeth and Ryan included in their wedding program an announcement that their wedding was "a carbon neutral event." "I didn't want to make a big display of it," she says, "but on the other hand I wanted to tell people so they think about it." She realizes some guests might perceive their efforts as being over the top. Of all the green elements in their wedding, she concedes, carbon offsets were among the hardest for some people to grasp.

"I haven't told my parents yet," Elizabeth said five months before the wedding. "They rolled their eyes when I mentioned an organic menu, so I imagine there'll be more eye rolling."

CHAPTER 8

THE RECEPTION
CAN I EAT THE POTATO FORK?

As a child growing up in Los Angeles in the 1970s, Stephanie Hibbert ate her share of canned soup. "There was no 'from the farm' experience back then," she notes. But at some point in adolescence, after visiting farmers' markets, Stephanie said she made the connection "between the people who grew the food and my plate. I just paid attention to what went into my body from a very early age."

Stephanie, 39, grew up to be an executive chef, one who took over the kitchen of one of the country's first planners of sustainable events, Back to Earth, in the San Francisco Bay Area, and who designed the menu for her own wedding. So when Stephanie married her longtime boyfriend, Mark Pearson, 35, in 2007 before 150 guests at Casa de La Vista, a former officer's club on Treasure Island, she was not only celebrating her love, but showcasing her culinary talents.

"The challenge was the diverse population," she says of feeding her guests. "It's a combination of wanting to show off what I do and having them feel very comfortable."

FOOD

Stephanie's menu (see "The Chef's Special" on page 128) was unconventional in some ways. She wanted a mix of comfort food, like a meatball appetizer, and some favorite foods, like the oyster bar for the oyster-loving groom. And she threw in a few dazzlers like her addictive "Mash-tinis," mashed potatoes served in martini glasses and topped with dill cashew crème, wild mushroom duxelle (finely chopped mushrooms sautéed with shallots and herbs), and fried shallots and chives.

But in its seasonal, local, and organic nature, Stephanie's menu reflected the preferred choice of more and more Americans when it comes to food and other consumer products. The produce and the chicken for the wedding came from organic farms no farther than 100 to 150 miles away. The type of fish was picked out of the Monterey Bay Aquarium's list of "ocean-friendly" seafood (see "Good Food" on page 133). To Stephanie, organic means no pesticides damaging the earth or the health of farm workers, and a throwback to the more

THE CHEF'S SPECIAL
AN EXECUTIVE CHEF'S MENU FOR HER OWN WEDDING

What does an organic chef serve at her own wedding? Stephanie and Mark's pirate-themed wedding featured an organic seasonal menu designed by the bride herself. This is what she chose.

PASSED HORS D'OEUVRES

Mango ceviche with avocado crème on slices of cucumber

Herb meatball brochettes with mushroom redux

Mash-tinis, or mashed yellow-fin potatoes topped with dill cashew crème, wild mushroom duxelle, and fried shallots and chives, served in martini glasses

Oyster bar, with sustainably raised oysters from Tomales Bay

DINNER

Caprese salad with heirloom tomatoes, mozzarella, and fresh basil and herbed olive oil, sprinkled with black sea salt

Vegetarian tart with maitake and other exotic mushrooms

Lemon herbed halibut

Pan-seared herbed chicken

Sides of broccoli rabe, saffron rice pilaf, and fresh-baked artisan bread

Pasta marinara (for kids)

DESSERT

Lemon cupcakes with meringue butter cream

Truffles (cinnamon-dusted, hazelnut-butter, and other flavors, made with organic chocolate)

BEVERAGES

Non-alcoholic strawberry lemonade, melon-mint cooler, herbal tisane tea, and Fair Trade coffee

Organic wine from Frey Vineyards

Beer

natural way we used to farm. "When you see an organic cucumber you see a twisted up cucumber," she says approvingly.

Times have changed, and any foray into the grocery store now yields organic options for pretty much everything you may wish to eat. (Be ready to put up with some organic shtick, too. "This is pizza with integrity," the box for my frozen "American Flatbread" pizza reads.) Grown without most conventional pesticides or petroleum-based or sewage sludge-based fertilizers—and with the animals given no growth hormones or antibiotics—organic food is undoubtedly easier on the environment than conventional fare. Some argue that it is also healthier for consumers, but the debate on that issue continues, with some people questioning whether organic products are worth their higher price.

Finding an organic caterer should not be hard. Even caterers who don't bill themselves as strictly organic can come up with an organic menu following your wishes, although it would be better to find someone who already has relationships with organic farms. Scan caterers' websites to find out the kinds of ingredients they use. Another way to search: Go to your farmers' market and ask organic farmers which local restaurants and caterers buy from them.

Seasonal ingredients are just as important—you don't want your veggies from heated greenhouses in the winter. And local food also minimizes the toll on the environment by cutting back on the transportation. Products that travel long distances require more packaging and refrigeration as well.

But there's a gray area. Some studies have suggested that how far the food has traveled (known as "food miles") should not be the only consideration. A 2006 study by Lincoln University in New Zealand, for example, found that lamb, apples, and onions shipped from New Zealand to the United Kingdom generated fewer greenhouse gas emissions overall than if the same products had originated in Europe. Why? Better energy efficiency in New Zealand during the growing and production process. Shoppers, of course, have no way of measuring emissions for every product, even if they walked around with a calculator. So until the time comes when the cost of travel-related pollution is built into the price of products, you may want to avoid off-season menu ingredients shipped great distances. If you build your menu around what is grown nearby, you also help your local economy. (See "Good Food" on page 133.)

To go even greener in selecting your wedding menu, avoid meat, especially beef. A raw menu or a vegan menu of fruits, veggies, grains, and nuts may be too extreme for some weddings, but the argument for cutting back on meat to protect the environment from needless damage is powerful. A report by the United Nations Food and Agriculture Organization in 2006 included the startling finding that the livestock business, or raising animals for meat, generates more greenhouse gases than all forms of transportation combined. One reason is that in some countries there has been massive deforestation to clear pasture land for cattle. Another reason is that huge volumes of methane gas and nitrous oxide are produced in animal manure and the gas they pass.

ABOVE An autumnal display of organic pies replaces the traditional wedding cake at Kelly Nichols' reception. Drinks were served in recyclable cups.

ABOVE Home-baked shortbread biscuits with fresh berries finished off the meal at Ben and Margo's reception. It began with local baby carrots, asparagus, and mushrooms.

So if you must serve meat, poultry is preferred. Stick to just one meat item. And if you go with fish, make sure you are avoiding overfished species, or fish farmed in ways detrimental to the environment and other marine life. And, of course, avoid big fish that have a high mercury content. (See "Good Food" on page 133.)

There is absolutely no reason for an organic menu to be any less delicious or inventive than a conventional spread. The wedding menu at the Inn of the Seventh Ray, an organic restaurant next to a creek in Topanga, California (and a favorite of mine), features dishes like Agave Glazed Vegan Duck, Wild Mushroom Risotto and Roast Beet with Crème Fraîche. But Eric Fenster, co-owner of Back to Earth, notes organic food can cost anywhere from 20 to 100 percent more because growing it is generally more labor intensive—more labor is required to manage pests without conventional pesticides, for example. Also, conventional farming enjoys government subsidies that help keep prices low. Organic production is also limited by rules such as the ban on hormones that conventional farmers use on cows to boost their milk production.

That's why, during a shopping trip, a conventional chicken breast at Safeway went for $3.49/lb while Roxie Organic Chicken breast wholesale was priced at $7/lb. Similarly, the conventional asparagus went for $3.99/lb, compared with $6.99/lb for organic asparagus at the same supermarket.

Still, many couples find the cost well worth it, even when going green requires some adjustments. For instance, when using only seasonal produce, you won't be able to do off-season tastings. And because organic production is so much at the mercy of Mother Nature, unpredictable shortages may affect what's available for the wedding. These are all hurdles that can be overcome, however.

Stephanie, who does tastings for her clients four to nine months in advance on average, advises couples to ask their caterer what substitutions can be made if, for instance, peaches aren't looking good or if the asparagus crop was smaller than expected. As the chef, she suggests substitutions. "You need to trust your chef and be flexible," she says. Stephanie also notes that in creating an organic kitchen, "it's not just produce. It's spices and beans and sugars. You need to back it up with all this, otherwise it's just part organic."

But she concedes some products pose dilemmas. She says some farms she likes are in transition to organic practices but have not yet won certification from the Department of Agriculture. It usually takes years for farms to meet the strict organic certification standards, as they clear chemicals from the soil, for example. But Stephanie says she doesn't hesitate to buy from such producers because "these are farmers who need our support before they are certified organic."

"If we only supported the mega farms that are organic, the smaller farms wouldn't survive," she says.

DRINK

"Organic" goes well beyond fresh foods. You can find certified organic wines, beers, tequilas, vodkas, and mixers. Biodynamic wines (which carry the Demeter certification label) are also arriving on wine lists at even top restaurants. For our third wedding anniversary in 2008, my husband and I enjoyed a 2005 biodynamic chardonnay from Brick House Vineyards in Oregon that wine critic Robert Parker compared to a French premier Cru burgundy. Green never tasted so good.

You'll find plenty of organic beer and wine producers from the United States and Europe, and there is excellent organic sparkling wine, such as cava from Spain, prosecco from Italy, and biodynamic Champagne from France. Paolo Bonetti, president of Organic Vintners in Boulder, Colorado, says consumers should avoid vague labels, such as those reading "sustainable wine," and look for certified organic instead. (These labels include "USDA Organic," "Made with organic grapes," and "Organic wine," depending on the levels of sulfites.) Try out the offerings of Frey Vineyards, which carries both organic and biodynamic wines that are found in stores nationwide at reasonable prices. OrganicVintners.com carries organic wines and sparkling wines from nine countries, including the United States, France, and Chile, and ships directly to consumers in states that allow out-of-state purchases.

For beer, check for organic brands such as Vermont-based Wolaver's organic ales or Butte Creek Brewing, sold in liquor stores and at Whole Foods and other supermarkets around the country. A neat idea some couples try: having a local micro-brewery brew an organic beer in your name.

Tea and coffee are available from Fair Trade Certified companies like Green Mountain Coffee Roasters (www.GreenMountainCoffee.com), Alter Eco (www.AlterEcoUSA.com), and Numi Organic Tea (www.NumiTea.com).

Among the selections at Organic Vintners: a 2005 vegan blend of Grenache, Cabernet Sauvignon, and Syrah from Spain made with certified organic grapes.

Seasonal. Local. Organic. Eco-friendly. To find it in your area, check the following websites:

◎ The Natural Resources Defense Council (www.nrdc.org) has a list of fresh produce available by state and by season. Explore the site's "Health" section for other information, such as the "hot list" of commonly air-freighted foods to avoid, like asparagus from Peru and bell peppers from the Netherlands.

◎ For farmers' markets and family farms, try www. LocalHarvest.org and www. EatWellGuide.org.

◎ The Environmental Working Group (www.ewg.org) has a ranking of fruits and veggies by pesticide "load," based on the results of tests collected by the Department of Agriculture and the Food and Drug Administration between 2000 and 2004.

◎ For what fish to buy and why, try the Monterey Bay Aquarium's www.Seafoodwatch. org or the Environmental Defense Fund's seafood selector at www.edf.org. Check out the fish at www.Ecofish.com.

UNIQUE YET GREEN: A PIRATE WEDDING

Stephanie Anne Hibbert and Mark Michael Pearson—first introduced by their tattoo artists—picked a venue with breathtaking views of the Golden Gate Bridge and Alcatraz Island: the former officers' club on Treasure Island. "We deeply love this city and it is here where we found each other and fell in love," the

couple said on their wedding website. The spot also helped the couple unleash their playful sides. They chose a pirate theme, featuring treasure chests and skulls for centerpieces, rub-on tattoos as party favors, and a wedding program that described the event as a "festival/carnival/celebration."

No white taffeta gown for this bride. Stephanie wore black lace over white satin. She sported a nose ring, and her luxurious red hair cascaded down her back, a mane of curls and braids. Her bridesmaids wore goth black, some with matching black nail polish and fishnet stockings. Ari Derfel, co-owner of Back to Earth and a Universal Church minister, officiated wearing a pirate's outfit, complete with ruffled shirt and feathered hat, rented from a local theater company's wardrobe department.

Mark, the groom, chose a Johnny Cash–inspired "honky tonk"

suit, accessorized with a Stetson hat, bolo tie on black shirt, and cowboy boots. For a moment he looked as if he had landed in the wrong musical. But as the couple exchanged verses from popular love songs during the outdoor ceremony as a cool bay breeze tickled their faces, they were in complete synch. "You are the

sunshine of my life," Stephanie offered. "You don't have to be rich to be my girl," Mark replied.

On the back of the wedding program, under "caterer," it read: "Yes. This is Stephanie's crew. Aren't they lovely? We hope you enjoy a taste of her work." I did, since Stephanie and Mark had graciously allowed me to witness their wedding for my research. Served by a waitstaff who could have been extras from *Pirates of the Caribbean*, the food was as spectacular as the view of the San Francisco skyline.

Stephanie, who not long after the wedding left Back to Earth to start her own catering business as "Chef Stephanie, Culinary Mistress," and Mark, who worked on motorcycles sales, had been

true to many green precepts. They bought her engagement and wedding rings at a pawnshop. They posted their wedding invitation on their wedding website. They

rejected a pots-and-pans registry and suggested instead cash for their honeymoon in Thailand, where Stephanie had planned to take cooking classes.

For their wedding, they used attire they would wear again. They bought local flowers. They treated their guests to an organic feast. Whenever they could in planning their wedding, they made green choices.

As I watched Stephanie at the wedding party, glowing happily, laughing and mingling with her guests, I remembered something she had told me a few weeks before that made me realize how her food conveyed her strong values. "I consider myself to be a food activist," Stephanie told me. "My work is my activism."

TABLEWARE

For a holiday party we gave in early December 2007, I went online and ordered biodegradable plates, cups, napkins, and utensils from World Centric at WorldCentric. org, a nonprofit organization based in Palo Alto, California, that works to reduce environmental degradation. The cardboard-like plates were made of sugar cane fiber ("bagasse"), and the forks and knives, which felt like sturdy plastic, were made with starch from corn and potato. The night of the party, I discreetly tried to gauge my guests' reaction.

"My kids' school uses these," says Madeleine, the mother of elementary school twins, as she nibbled on

pasta from the oval-shaped plates. "Does this mean I can eat the fork?" quipped my friend Gabriel, an entertainment publicist in Hollywood.

No one batted an eye, and I became a convert to compostable disposables. But while perfect for casual celebrations, "most people having weddings feel the compostables just aren't elegant enough," Fenster, the organic food caterer, says. The choice for weddings is usually green: reusable china, stemware, and silverware from local rental places. One question you can ask is what kind of cleaning supplies they use, to make sure they have switched to nontoxic types.

Fenster advises couples to keep in mind some basics:

◎ The number of courses determines the amount of plates and other equipment required to be transported and washed. For the least impact, pare down the courses and choose a seated dinner rather than a buffet, which requires more plates and utensils when people go back for seconds.

◎ Serve just wine and beer and a signature cocktail like a mojito rather than a full bar, which requires seven different kinds of glasses.

◎ Ban bottled water to avoid the plastic and the energy required to deliver all those bottles. For all water needs at an event, Back to Earth brings a filter to hook up to the tap.

◎ Offer leftovers to the catering staff or send them to a soup kitchen so that nothing is wasted. Make arrangements to have scraps composted (try local gardens or city compost stations).

LET THEM EAT PIE:
THE ORGANIC CAKE AND ITS SWEET RIVALS

Francisco Machado, a pastry chef with Back to Earth, says the green market provides everything he needs to make a 100 percent organic wedding cake—flour, sugar, butter, eggs, milk, cream, cornstarch, chocolate, aluminum-free baking powder, and other ingredients. He also makes vegan cakes, such as his Vegan Maple Chocolate Cake, with tofu and maple syrup.

Machado decorates his cakes with a smooth coating of meringue buttercream and crystallized mint leaves or whole fruit. He combines soymilk, tofu, lemon juice, palm shortening, and powdered sugar for the frosting. Inn of the Seventh Ray, an organic restaurant in Topanga Canyon, near

Los Angeles, makes cakes with whole wheat flours, fruit sweeteners, and nut flavors from the kitchen's own roasted nuts. For frosting they use whipped cream or whipped tofu.

An organic cake may have a champagne or "off white" color because organic butter tends to be yellowish, Machado notes, but you won't be short-changed on flavor.

"You can make really delicious organic cakes," he says, citing an organic marzipan creation for a recent wedding. "The most important factor is, how fresh is your cake? Most organic food tastes better, in my opinion."

Many couples, however, forgo the traditional wedding cake for more playful organic fare, such as:

◎ Finger food and bite-size desserts like truffles, tartlets, petit fours, and mini-cupcakes.

◎ Scoops of sorbet in martini glasses.

◎ Cookies and biscotti dipped in an organic chocolate fountain.

◎ Pies. At the wedding of Kelly Nichols and Alan Puccinelli in Northern California, guests feasted on trays of pies, including strawberry, pecan, freshly picked apples and pumpkin. A friend of the family made them in glass dishes bought from a Salvation Army thrift store and set them, seven at a time, on round trays on a cake table. They were organized in a tiered design adorned with pumpkins and other autumn decorations appropriate for the October 2007 celebration.

For cake toppers and decorative touches, plastic is out at most green weddings. Karin Ascot and Patrick Van Haren of Austin decorated their three-tiered cake with fresh roses and baby's breath.

SWAG

A few months before their May 2008 wedding, Katie Malouf and Joe Bous of Washington, D.C., were thinking of making a donation to organizations that help workers in Colombia's flower industry. Goodbye party favor.

"I hate the idea of crystal trinkets that people don't know what to do with," says Katie, who planned to make the donation on behalf of her guests. "There's also the

The reception table makes room for the green party favor: donations to the couple's favorite cause.

extreme of sending people home with their own personal mini-wedding cake. I've stopped reading bride magazines."

Wedding etiquette says party favors are optional, and many couples with a green mindset are opting out of silly trinkets and disposables. We all have politely dragged those home and then simply tossed them, haven't we? "We didn't want to add to the consumerism," says Patrick Van Haren, who offered no party favors when he married Karin Ascot in October of 2006 in a park in Austin, Texas.

But many couples still want to offer party favors, just not to their guests. Instead, they are donating to favorite causes so that everyone can share in the gesture of making a positive contribution. Lesley and Jason Whyard, of New Jersey, were on a tight budget for their April 2007 wedding, so they called up the World Wildlife Fund to make a $100 donation in honor of their 120 guests. Every little bit helps.

"I just see so much waste in favors, like $3 for votive candles," says Lesley, who placed small cards announcing the donation between plates at the banquet hall. "If we're going to put money toward it, why not put money on something useful?"

For party favors with a purpose, try:

◎ **PHILANTHROPIC FAVORS**. From the World Wildlife Fund (which also offers symbolic animal adoptions and gift memberships) to the American Diabetes Association, scores of organizations are happy to help you add value to your wedding. Also try ABC Carpet & Home's foundation (www.abchomeandplanet.org), which has a line of "gifts of compassion."

You can also tie the favors to the venue by, for example, donating a flower bulb in the name of each guest to the botanical garden where you wed.

◎ **PRACTICAL FAVORS**. At Haily Zaki and Brian Tuey's wedding celebration at a campsite in Southern California, the couple gave recycled brown paper goodie bags containing oblong pillows made by the bride's mom for 30 friends to sit on around the fire. The bags also included granola bars and snacks in case guests got hungry in the middle of the night.

Kelly Nichols and Alan Puccinelli of California offered throw blankets made out of recycled materials. The blankets, placed over the backs of chairs at their outdoor wedding, came in handy when temperatures dipped.

◎ **EDIBLES**. Remember the almonds wrapped in tulle? We've come a long way. Find out where to buy bird-friendly "shade grown coffee," grown in the shade of tropical forest trees to help conserve them, from the Smithsonian Institution at www.NationalZoo.si.edu/ConservationAndScience/MigratingBirds/Coffee. For chocolate mini-bars, try Fair Trade Certified chocolates from DivineChocolate.com or TheoChocolate.com. For a real conversation piece, give insect candy from www.Hotlix.com. And for local gifts that don't require shipping, go with local artisans or get jars of

LEFT Cosmetic tote with a striped pattern, crafted by artisans in India who recycle the colorful plastic bags that litter the streets of New Delhi. (From World of Good)

RIGHT Sandalwood fans with antique velvet ribbons help keep guests cool, then become take-home gifts.

jam or honey from a local farm (at one wedding, the jars read "To the sweet life").

◎ **CRAFTS**. Do you paint or draw? You can share your art with a captive audience. Even if you're not crafty, enlist friends who are and have them make watercolors or ceramic mugs for party favors. Also, you can give paper a new life as a flower with plantable boxes that can hold a gift such as flower seeds (see www.CustomPaper.com).

Gifts for the bridal party should be a little more upscale—vintage charms, gift card sets in seed-embedded handmade paper, baskets of organic personal care products (try www.EccoBella.com), or organic wine are all suitable presents. Kelly Nichols gave her bridesmaids necklaces that she and her sister made, among other handcrafted gifts. You can find earrings, necklaces, and bracelets and other Fair Trade handicrafts from World of Good (www.WorldofGoodInc.com), which showcases the work of hundreds of artisan cooperatives around the world.

And remember: Some guests take a plane back home or face hours on the road after the party, so gifts should travel well.

ABOVE Unwrapped gifts for the groomsmen.

MUSIC

At Inn of the Seventh Ray, an organic and biodynamic restaurant in Topanga Canyon near Los Angeles, they don't do rap or rock. DJs can play softer rhythms as long as they don't blare the music and interfere with the ebb and flow of the conversations. Owner Lucile S. Yaney, a psychotherapist who believes in the power of vibrations, says music should harmonize with the surroundings, which at this beautifully rustic restaurant includes a canopy of sycamores and oaks alongside Topanga Creek.

"If they're keeping with the philosophy of harmonious co-existence, they'd have classical," Yaney says of marrying couples. "You keep your music as pure as possible." Classical music fits in perfectly with a green wedding, but you don't have to be a traditionalist by any means. Flamenco guitars, mariachi bands, and even Caribbean

steel drummers can be suitable depending on the celebration, says Michael Caldwell, co-founder of Gigmasters.com, a web-based booking service for live music and entertainment. Since 2007, he says, demand for soloists and ensembles that require no amplification—meaning they need no power, a green plus—has significantly risen, specially for harpists and acoustic guitarists. "They create a peaceful atmosphere," Caldwell says.

Whether you are trying to avoid rattling the natural environment or you want to conserve energy, try:

◎ Replacing the organ and other electricity-powered instruments for the ceremony with acoustic music, such as a string quartet or a singer accompanied by her guitar.

◎ Replacing the dance band for the reception with an iPod, whether a DJ's or your own. With the compact iPod sound system you can easily feature your play lists and those of your guests if you solicit music requests ahead of time and download them for the wedding. Acoustic music also works for smaller parties, with, say, fewer than one hundred guests—for example, a steel drum band for a beach wedding or strolling mariachis for venues both indoors and out.

At Inn of the Seventh Ray in Topanga Canyon, near Los Angeles, organic and biodynamic food is served alongside a creek under a canopy of sycamores and oaks.

Musical instruments await the party inside a barn. In the background, a salvaged section of a redwood.

The Baguette Quartette plays Parisian music at Francis Ford Coppola's Rubicon Estate in Napa Valley.

CHAPTER 9

THE ECO-HONEYMOON
PLEASE, NO BUGS

During their trip to Thailand in November 2007, newlyweds Jen Belbis and Eric Bassik chopped bamboo with machetes and frolicked with kids at an orphanage. They even slept at the orphanage, ten people to a room, not counting the uninvited guests: mosquitoes the size of flies. How's that for a honeymoon?

"It was life changing," says Eric, 30, a television account executive with a media management company in Los Angeles. "It was great to give a hand to other people in need."

Honeymoons conjure up images of romantic locales, like Paris, or a beach resort along the pristine waters of some secluded Caribbean island. But many newlyweds are looking for more meaningful experiences. A perfect way to segue from your green wedding to a green honeymoon is through ecotourism. Tourist destinations are too often associated with pollution, waste, and rampant development. The goal of ecotourism is to use your tourist dollars to actually help protect the environment.

The idea of ecologically sound tourism has existed for decades, but it got a big push when the United Nations declared 2002 "the International Year of Ecotourism."

Jen Belbis, in green, and other volunteers pass out candy and art supplies to orphaned Thai children after school.

Eco-travel soon became one of the fastest-growing trends, with new destinations popping up all over the map, beyond East Africa, Australia, Costa Rica and other traditional ecotourism spots. In fact, you may find ecotourism closer than you might think, a circumstance that does the environment good because it means you would produce fewer transportation-related carbon emissions by traveling less and probably staying longer, a trend known as "slow travel."

Tourism that doesn't adversely affect the environment or the local population is sold under many names—"cultural," "adventure," "sustainable," "ethical," "geotourism," "voluntourism," and others. But for it to be true ecotourism, says The International Ecotourism Society, or TIES, a travel industry organization, it should involve responsible travel to natural areas that helps conserve the environment and improve the well-being of local people.

Under this definition, an all-inclusive cruise that does not put money in local hands or city travel that has no focus on nature would not be "eco." At its core, says Kelly Bricker, chair of the TIES board, "ecotourism is really about interacting with nature. You're staying in an eco-lodge that's not in downtown Los Angeles."

But an eco-honeymoon doesn't necessarily require trekking through a jungle or not showering for three days. "Eeeoww!" some newlyweds would say. Eco-tourist destinations both at home and overseas run the gamut, from those offering luxurious comfort, even in a tree house, to budget travel options that don't necessarily require roughing it.

Destinations and tours that promote environmental education and responsibility are multiplying fast. It is happening in countries and areas as varied as El Salvador, Wisconsin, the Fiji Islands, Gambia, and Bali. While countries promote their parks, wildlife, and other natural resources, hotels and resorts have been rushing to install their own green features—geothermal energy, dual-flush toilets, organic cotton sheets. My husband and I have become regulars at the Copamarina Beach Resort, a one-hundred-plus-room property in Puerto Rico, in the southwestern town of Guanica, that is minutes away from a subtropical dry forest that has been named a United Nations Biosphere Reserve to conserve its ecosystem.

The hotel, like more and more hotels, launders linens every three days unless a guest objects. But Copamarina also recycles all its paper, plastics, glass, and water. It takes leftover food from its two restaurants to a pig farm. It has installed low-flow toilets and energy-efficient lighting, and it was looking into solar power. Hotel employees also have a "green team" that has adopted a local school and that clears a nearby beach of debris washed into the ocean by two nearby rivers.

Nestled between the ocean and a subtropical dry forest in Guanica, Puerto Rico, the Copamarina Beach Resort is one of the island's green hotels.

The view from one of the trails of Guanica's dry forest, a United Nations Biosphere Reserve.

Copamarina's reasonable rates seem to reflect the savings from its green measures, but many ecotourism packages are high-end and pricey—as in $600 a night in some cases. But budget options abound, including the ideal eco-honeymoon closer to home. While the United States has lagged behind in marketing attractions as ecotourism, it is catching up. The national park system is the grand jewel of American ecotourism, from the subtle beauty of Joshua Tree National Park in the desert of Southern California to the alligator-friendly Everglades in South Florida. Faced with bigger crowds and environmental degradation, the National Park Service has worked at becoming more green in recent years by reducing energy consumption, increasing recycling, and other efforts. Parks like Zion National Park in Utah are leading the way, with lodges that offer organic food, do their own composting, and landscape with water-efficient plants.

But you can practice ecotourism no matter the destination by the way you behave as a traveler (for more on this see "The Eco-Tourist, Anywhere" on page 152). Are you putting money in local hands by hiring local guides and supporting family-run businesses? Are you taking the bus to explore the town, or better yet, biking, horseback riding, or walking? Are you buying souvenirs not made in China (unless you're in China)? Are you preparing for your trip by learning a few words in the native language and some local customs?

This is not difficult to do, and your honeymoon can be just as sweet, if not sweeter.

THE ECO-TOURIST, ANYWHERE:
PRACTICING ECOTOURISM NO MATTER WHERE YOU GO

Ecotourism is not just enjoying some paradise on earth. How travelers behave on their trips makes a difference to the earth.

◎ Avoid air travel as much as you can, and buy carbon credits to offset such travel. The International Ecotourism Society recommends buying credits that support reforestation and energy conservation programs from ClimateCare at www.ClimateCare.org (see Chapter 7: The Guests for other recommendations).

◎ Ask yourself, "Who does my money benefit?" When you patronize local businesses, your money goes to the local economy and gives your hosts more reasons to appreciate and conserve their natural resources.

◎ Choose vendors who follow your green principles. Do they hire locally and have a small footprint themselves? If the lodge has a sprawling golf course, or the tour's educational component is a night at the casino, you may want to keep looking. Ask for their environmental policy.

◎ Do no harm. Bike, walk, or take public transportation to minimize carbon emissions while traveling. Learn about local traditions and practices to avoid giving offense. Do not touch (coral), perturb (animals), or take anything (plants, artifacts) along the way as you go sightseeing.

◎ Don't buy ancient artifacts or crafts or products made from protected or endangered animals.

◎ If bargaining, pay a fair price.

◎ Contribute to actual projects and research by traveling with nonprofit groups that design wilderness expeditions and other trips to raise money for their causes. Try the Nature Conservancy (www.Nature. org), Sierra Club Outings (www. SierraClub.org/outings), or Earthwatch Institute (www. Earthwatch.org).

◎ To become an effective eco-tourist, check out the United Nations Environment Programme's "Green Passport" guide at www.uneptie.org.

◎ Ethical Traveler (www. EthicalTraveler.org), a project of the Earth Island Institute in San Francisco, offers tips on how to act like a freelance "ambassador." ("Never give gifts to children," only to their parents or teachers, to discourage begging. "Never open an umbrella in a Nepali home," which is considered an insult because it implies that the house is in poor condition.)

ECOTOURISM EQUALS GOOD (FOR THE MOST PART)

The United States Agency for International Development, which gives aid to countries worldwide, has found that ecotourism fosters appreciation for natural resources in developing countries and leads to better conservation practices. Ecotourism has deterred logging in rain forests in Sierra Leone; protected fisheries in Fiji, Indonesia, and the Philippines; spurred reforestation programs in Thailand; and stopped plans for a coal power plant near undeveloped areas in Malaysia. Eco-tourists, and the

A volunteer works on a deep-sea mural at a home for street kids near São Paolo in Brazil.

revenue they bring, can make the difference between turning a tropical forest into cow pastures in places like Costa Rica or keeping it intact as a tourist attraction. And tourism in general plays a major role in reducing poverty in many countries.

"We need to support ecotourism," says Dr. Meg Lowman, a professor of biology and environmental studies at New College of Florida and vice president for education at the Ecological Society of America. "It's a great conservation tool."

While it is good that the ecotourism industry is growing by leaps and bounds, there is a catch—little towns or remote villages that open up to tourists sometimes grow too fast for their own good. And sometimes areas don't get around to imposing the regulations needed to control tourist-related construction and traffic to fragile areas, or to keep an eye on opportunistic tour operators. Conservation efforts can also suffer from lack of money.

"Without proper planning and laws and the structure in place to protect that area, it can get out of control," concedes Kelly Bricker, of TIES, who does research on sustainable tourism and travel as an associate professor in the Department of Parks, Recreation, and Tourism at the University of Utah. "You can find that all over the world, so we struggle with how much to market a certain area."

With ecotourism a hot buzzword in travel, take your time picking the right vendor (See "Where to Go First" on page 155). Don't fall for the pretty poster of a waterfall. If the resort's draw is great water-skiing, with its accompanying motorized boats, or 5,000 acres of golf courses, which not only consume great amounts of water but most likely sit on what was once a natural area, keep looking, advises Dr. Lowman. "You can tell by the activities offered if they are serious about educating people," she says. Check what's behind the "eco" advertising to make sure its not a marketing ruse. And watch out for overpaying for anything "eco."

By 2008, there was no uniform global certification for eco-tours, lodging, and services. One reason may be that there's much debate about the application of the term "eco." "Some people would argue zoos are ecotourism," notes Bricker. "I think it's a stretch, but there's an argument for that."

At the very least, try to look for a minimum commitment from tour operators, hotels, and other travel businesses. Do they minimize harm to the environment, hire locally, and educate visitors on the natural attractions?

One important thing to keep in mind: to get to those destinations travelers fly, drive, or use other motorized modes of transportation, spewing more greenhouse gases into the atmosphere. A United Nations report on climate change and tourism in 2007 estimated that tourism accounts for about 5 percent of all carbon dioxide emissions in the world. In one of life's cruel ironies, tourism both contributes to global warming and suffers because of it. Already, global warming is threatening tourist destinations all over the world, from the polar regions and the Alps to Glacier National Park in Montana and the always fragile marshlands of the Everglades, which are affected by rising sea levels and tropical storms.

So spend a little more and try to minimize the adverse impact of travel through carbon offsets now offered by many online booking websites as well as individual airlines and car rental companies. (See Chapter 7: The Guests for more on carbon offsets.) Dr. Lowman notes, however, that the value of ecotourism in helping countries appreciate the economic bonanza of conserving natural resources can not be underestimated. "It's a real important message, and it really supersedes the air travel issue," she says.

Honeymooners help out at a home for single mothers and their children in Suva, Fiji.

Browsing the Internet for buzz-words like "sustainable travel" or "ecotourism" may give you weeks' worth of research. Here's a list to get you started.

◎ The International Ecotourism Society, at www.ecotourism.org, lists tour operators, hotels, and lodges that have signed on to the organization's "code of conduct" for responsible travel.

◎ www.ResponsibleTravel.com offers eco-honeymoon packages and traveler reviews.

◎ www.SustainableTravel International.org offers carbon offset programs.

◎ www.Planeta.com has practical information about ecotourism.

◎ The Rainforest Alliance, www.rainforest-alliance.org, has an "eco-index" of sustain-able tourism businesses in Latin America and the Caribbean.

◎ A list of the world's most socially and environmen-tally ethical destinations can be found at Ethical Traveler, an advocacy group, at www.EthicalTraveler.org/destinations.

◎ In the United States, the National Park Service joined forces with the Environmental Protection Agency to give parks technical assistance to reduce carbon emissions and educate visitors about climate change. For a list of "climate friendly parks," like Yosemite in California and Glacier Bay in Alaska, go to www.nps.gov.

◎ In urban areas, visitors can find hotels that subscribe to environmental standards. Look for the seal of approval from the United States Green Building Council (www.usgbc.org), which offers LEED certification. To find hotels rated for their green practices, such as composting and gray water recycling, go to EnvironmentallyFriendlyHotels.com. Hotels that have shown interest in adopting green practices join the Green Hotels Association (www.GreenHotels.com).

◎ For well-regarded travel guides, try *Lonely Planet*, *Rough Guides*, and *Moon*.

◎ For an online sustainable travel magazine, go to www.Worldsurface.com

LOVEBIRDS WHO BIKE AND VOLUNTEER:
HOW TWO COUPLES HONEYMOONED

Who says you can't spend your honeymoon biking up and down cliffs for miles and miles a day? After their green wedding in the fall of 2007, Kelly Nichols and Alan Puccinelli of Danville, California, wanted a green but athletic honeymoon. They chose a ten-day bike tour of Croatia with Backroads, a travel company, taking boats from island to island to pedal the rugged coastline, often uphill. The trip, which was partly financed by their wedding registry, was not marketed as ecotourism, Kelly says, but it came with many green elements. The newlyweds pedaled 200 miles along the Dalmatian Coast of Croatia. They stayed in small B&Bs and mom-and-pop lodges. They sampled the local fish and Italian- and Greek-influenced cuisine and mingled with local people.

Croatia itself, a product of the 1990s wars that broke up Yugoslavia, seemed to follow

green principles, mostly out of necessity, Kelly notes. "They just reuse everything. Nothing is thrown away. It's part of their lifestyle. It seemed like everybody made their own wine and olive oils," she says. "We went to one woman's home and she bottled some olive oil for us in an old plastic Coke bottle."

Jen and Eric, another California couple, initially were not in

agreement about their unconventional honeymoon. Eric says he had been hesitant when Jen, 29, a toy company marketing analyst, suggested the working honeymoon trip to Thailand. He had been thinking along the lines of the Greek Isles or Hawaii. She wanted hands-on cultural immersion.

"I wanted to do volunteer work and learn more about Thai culture," says Jen, who had spent several spring breaks as a college student working with Habitat for Humanity, the nonprofit housing organization, in places like New Orleans and West Virginia. "Parts of Thailand are very touristy and you don't feel like you're getting an authentic experience."

Jen and Eric booked through Hands Up Holidays (www. HandsUpHolidays.com), a British travel operator. Christopher Hill, who launched the company in London in 2006, says his inspiration came from his own experience teaching English in Guatemala and Thailand, building houses in South Africa and Fiji, and participating in environmental projects in New Zealand and Thailand.

"I love exploring a country, but found that the most fulfilling and rewarding experiences took place when I contributed in a hands-on way to a community," Hill, a former investment banker, told me. "Hands Up Holidays was conceived to make it easy for people to have a holiday and a taste of volunteering, and hopefully get inspired to do more volunteering, either back at home, or on future trips, or both."

Some Hands Up Holidays trips are more "eco" than others. A trip to the Sunderbans in India, for example, focuses on mangrove planting and dyke maintenance in a community that, Hill says, "has been transformed from tiger poaching to tiger conservation through responsible, sustainable tourism." Other volunteer work can involve teaching, doing repairs in schools and hospitals, and harvesting crops.

Voluntourism, however, does not come cheap. Hands Up's trips deemed suitable for honeymooners start at $2,900 per person—for nine days in Fiji, including three of volunteer work, for example— and can go as high as $25,000, for eighteen days in New Zealand, with 4½ working days.

Jen and Eric spent four days in a seaside village north of Phuket that had been devastated by the tsunami of 2004. They helped artisans at a craft shop whose proceeds went to an orphanage for children who had lost their parents in the tragedy or whose

families could not support them. Jen and Eric spent time at the orphanage passing out after-school snacks and playing hand games and hide-and-seek with the children, up to age fifteen. As a parting gift, the couple bought the orphanage what it needed the most at the time—a washing machine.

They went on to five days of a more traditional vacation, including a jungle excursion and a couple of days in Bangkok all by themselves. "As long as you expect not to be surrounded by luxurious accommodations all the time, and your heart is in it, you'll be fine," Jen advises other newlyweds considering a similar honeymoon. "To meet the locals and understand their stories of survival, that was the best part." Eric says the experience left him humble and thankful—not a bad way to start his new married life.

"You appreciate the things that you have," he says. "I couldn't have asked for a better trip."

CHAPTER 10

THE LIFETIME COMMITMENT
HAPPILY GREEN EVER AFTER

After all that work, the wedding was fabulous. Congratulations! Friends and relatives are still talking about how much fun they had. You're proud that the celebration reflected your earth-restoring values (see Epilogue on page 173). Now you and your spouse can settle into married life with a sense of shared mission, of common purpose. Now is the time to make a smooth transition from your green vows to a green lifestyle, and reap a lifetime of rewards. Marriage in itself is good for the environment. Two people share land, energy, and other resources, consuming less than they would separately. Still, there is plenty of room for more efficiencies in your love nest.

Our Christmas lights, our heated bathrooms, our air conditioned offices, our garbage—they all produce greenhouse gases in enormous volume. But you can control that. Energy Star light fixtures, appliances, home electronics, and heating and cooling products reduced greenhouse gas emissions in 2006 by the equivalent of the annual output of pollutants of 25 million cars, according to the Environmental Protection Agency and the

Solar power, bamboo floors, dual-flush toilets and easy access to public transportation are among the green features of these stylish LEED-certified town homes from Olson Homes in Orange, California.

Department of Energy, which jointly run the program at www.EnergyStar.gov.

So your home is the perfect place to start reducing personal C02 emissions, and often saving money in the process. The Big Three sources of greenhouse gas emissions from the home are electricity use, heating, and waste. The environment inside homes can also become dangerously polluted. The EPA says indoor pollution—a result of formaldehyde in the carpets, mold hidden in walls and damp closets, and radon gas in basements and under the homes (go to the American Lung Association's www.HealthHouse.org to learn more)—can be two-to-three times higher than outdoor levels and lead to asthma and other illnesses. As a result, one critical element in greening your home involves nothing more than providing adequate ventilation, as well as using nontoxic caulks and sealants, building materials that inhibit mildew and mold, and paints with low or zero V.O.C., the hazardous chemicals known as volatile organic compounds.

Many of us have already made simple changes such as switching to compact fluorescent bulbs, which last far longer than incandescent bulbs and require a fraction of the energy. But many Americans now realize the importance of taking more ambitious steps. (To calculate your current personal emissions, go to websites like www.epa.gov/climatechange/emissions/individual.html or Global Footprint Network's www.FootprintCalculator.org.)

Some of us have been hurried along by extraordinary circumstances. In June 2005, Karin Ascot's home in Austin, Texas, a wood-framed house built in the 1900s, burned to the ground after a painter accidentally started

a fire during some renovations. Like Scarlett O'Hara in *Gone with the Wind*, Karin, 39, a German-English translator, was far from defeated. She turned adversity to advantage after she married Patrick Van Haren, 40, an entrepreneur in renewable energy projects. The couple decided not just to rebuild but to construct a new home that would be as green as their wedding.

"It was a disaster that my home went up in flames, but there's a huge silver lining," says Karin, who had a potluck wedding celebration at Zilker Metropolitan Park in Austin in October 2006. "By building a green home we're controlling a lot more of what happens in the home environment where we spend most of our life."

Karin and Patrick hired an architect, but they made the home building project their own. Karin says she subscribed to magazines like *Natural Home* for ideas. She read *The New Natural House Book* by David Pearson. The couple also followed the building guidelines of the city of Austin, which encourages residents to go green by offering rebates for steps that save energy. Karin and Patrick aimed for the city's highest green rating, five stars, for the two buildings on their property—a main house and a two-story, 1,600-square-foot building with an apartment and the couple's offices.

TOP Solar panels on the roof capture sunlight to generate electricity for Karin and Patrick's home in Austin, Texas. **BOTTOM** Windows face away from the summer heat.

GREEN HOMES

Karin and Patrick's planning started out with the solar orientation of the house, which in their location meant having most windows facing south and north to avoid some of the scorching Texas heat in the summer. They planned to invest in a 25,000-gallon rainwater cistern for all their water, including drinking water. And they were tapping into the plentiful Texas sunshine to generate their own power.

In the United States, we have generated electricity mainly from fossil fuels, largely coal, or to a lesser extent from nuclear power plants and hydroelectric dams. But energy from the sun, wind, and other renewable sources, according to the EPA, "dramatically lowers pollution emissions, reduces environmental health risks, and slows the depletion of finite natural resources." Shifting to renewable sources of energy could be, experts say, the single most transformative step toward preventing greater global warming.

So for their electricity needs, Karin and Patrick were planning to get photovoltaic panels that rely on sunlight to generate power. They installed a solar water heater to warm water for the showers and other domestic needs. "Hydronic heating," which uses warmed water to heat the air, and radiant floor heating, which keeps the home toasty with little energy by warming the floors, completed their "solar thermal" system.

A stylish kitchen comes with cabinetry low in indoor air pollutants like formaldehyde.

Karin and Patrick, who had a baby boy, Theodore, on Halloween 2007, also made sure to use low V.O.C. paints. The kitchen cabinets and all the plywood had low formaldehyde concentrations and nontoxic finishes.

How difficult or expensive was it to build green? Major features like a metal roof that cools off faster in the evenings compared to traditional shingles, and lasts longer, were more expensive at the outset but would result in savings in the long term in the form of lower air conditioning costs, Karin says. The U.S. Green Building

Council, which administers the LEED (Leadership in Energy and Environmental Design) national standards for green construction, says green measures, depending on how far they go, can reduce energy consumption by 30 to 60 percent and water use by 20 to 50 percent.

Karin was looking forward to the savings once the construction was completed. In her old house, she says, she'd spend $80 to $120 a month for natural gas in heating. During one particularly cold month, the bill hit $365. Not anymore. "In our new house, with thermal heating, we won't even have a natural gas bill, and the electric bill will be well under $100," Karin calculated.

Most newlyweds aren't in a position to build new homes from scratch, of course. But they can green their existing homes, whether they are renters or homeowners (see "Calling Home Depot" on page 170) or decide to buy a new home that has already been greened. Southern California, where I live, has embraced the green home concept, partly because the region's air is among the most polluted in the nation and partly because a new culture of energy consciousness is taking hold. I've toured numerous houses, town houses, condos, and even pre-fabs that use green features as a powerful sales pitch. The homes come with stylish furnishings—countertops and floors made of bamboo, cork, or other renewable materials; recycled glass tiles; and "dual flush" toilets, which come with both a standard and a lighter flow.

But just like the tastefully designed green wedding, a green home is indistinguishable from any other gorgeous home. It takes close inspection to tell that there's a solar panel on the roof.

A modern design, built-in furniture, and modular millwork make this LEED-certified prefabricated home from Living Homes stand out in Santa Monica, California.

IT'S NOT ALL ABOUT SHOPPING

It's great that as individuals we're changing our lifestyles to reduce our carbon footprint, but coming together with others and organizing on a large scale to demand government action will have an even greater impact. Environmental leaders like former Vice President Al Gore urge us not to see our green purchases and practices as ends in themselves, but as complements to more concerted group action.

You can:

◎ Take steps to join the collective fight against global warming. Go to www.WeCanSolveIt.org, a project of Gore's The Alliance for Climate Protection, for ideas about how to advocate for change ("Call a talk radio show and speak your mind"). Commit to the movement inspired by the Live Earth concerts staged around the world by following the seven courses of action known as the "Live Earth Pledge" (www.LiveEarthPledge.org), including "to fight for laws and policies that expand the use of renewable energy sources and reduce dependence on oil and coal."

◎ Vote for political candidates who are committed to strong environmental laws.

◎ Join and support organizations fighting for environmental causes you feel strongly about. At the very least, go to their websites to add your name to their petitions and letter-writing campaigns.

◎ Invest in socially responsible projects. Look at your investment portfolio and steer your money toward investments that put money into facilities such as day cares and clinics, into affordable housing and environmental programs. What can beat a return that has both financial and social benefits? Look for mutual funds with socially responsible investment (SRI) options and, as an investor, insist that your companies do their share in fighting climate change and refusing to give money to polluters. To find SRI options, check the Community Investing Center (www.CommunityInvest.org), a project of the Social Investment Forum Foundation and Co-op America, two nonprofits working on social issues. Also try the United States Department of the Treasury's Community Development Financial Institutions Fund (www.cdfifund.gov/awardees/db/index.asp). For savings and money market accounts, there's www.CalvertFoundation.org and www.Domini.com. For mutual funds and their social criteria, check www.SocialInvest.org and www.SocialFunds.com.

THE GREEN LIFESTYLE

If you thought of a green wedding in the first place, chances are that you already eat organic foods, take mass transit to work, and recycle your refuse. Some changes are easy. Turning off computers and monitors when not in use. Running around a nearby park for exercise instead of driving to the gym. Washing clothes with cold water. For tougher changes, try to strike a balance.

"Do the things that are practical for you," says Susan Burns, managing director of Global Footprint Network in Oakland, California. "Perhaps riding your bike to work three times per week is easier than giving up fresh fruit in the winter months and will result in greater footprint savings on balance."

I've taken small steps for years but my real conversion came mid-way through the research of this book, when I attended a roving trade fair called Green Festival (known as Greenfest) in San Francisco, in a warehouse the size of a city block, crammed with thousands of people. The number and variety of products available was stunning— soy cashmere sweaters (nice), hemp chocolate milk (not so good) and organic wine and beer (as effective as nonorganic). It drew a diverse crowd in age and types of people, far from the "hippy dippy" and religious types that I was told used to provide the main audience for natural product fairs years ago. But devotees were still in evidence in the talks and panels, where speakers incited audiences to action on everything from composting to socially responsible investing. "The power of your money can make a difference!" "Let's grow the Fair Trade marketplace!"

"Go home, build your pile, and let it rot!"

In that spirit, here are some behavioral changes that matter the most:

COMMUTING. Don't be like California Governor Arnold Schwarzenegger—an environmental crusader in policy-making but who commuted by private jet to the state capital in Sacramento from his Los Angeles home nearly 400 miles away. Instead, avoid using your car by working from home, or telecommuting, whenever you can. Rely on buses and other mass transit, or car pooling, if available. If you drive, what you drive makes a difference. A 2008 Toyota Prius achieves a perfect 10 in the EPA greenhouse gas scores. By contrast, a 2008 Ford Expedition gets a score of 2. Use the EPA Green Vehicle Guide (www.epa.gov/greenvehicles) for comparisons and for making improvements, before the government forces us to tool around on Segway scooters.

SHOPPING. In one of the better pieces of news, the green living checklist is getting longer as the marketplace responds to demand for sustainable products. The green market extends to babies and pets. Green fever has taken over ads and marketing, from skin care creams touting their bio-dynamically grown ingredients to new green product lines at major retailers like Target and Home Depot, which has an "Eco Options" label for items that promote energy efficiency, clean water, and sustainable forestry.

Pay attention to third-party certification labels like "USDA Organic." Watch out for exorbitant prices for products sold as "earth-friendly." There's a premium for many green products, but they tend to stay in the range of 10 to 20 percent more costly than non-green equivalents, and prices should come down as more suppliers enter the market and demand swells. Shop around to make sure you're not a victim of unfair markups.

And beware of false health claims. In 2007, the athletic wear company Lululemon had to remove labels from shirts that made unreliable claims—such as the one that said the seaweed contained in the fabric "released marine amino acids, minerals, and vitamins into the skin," providing antibacterial, hydrating, and other benefits—that it could not prove.

You can find green guides and consumer websites to guide you, among them Co-op America's "National Green Pages" (www.GreenPages.org), a directory of environmentally and socially responsible products and services, and National Geographic Society's "Green Guide" (www.TheGreenGuide.com), which offers product recommendations, shopping suggestions, and reader ratings. Some guides offer local listings in major cities, such as Greenopia (www.Greenopia.com). Helpful websites include www.TreeHugger.com and www.WomenandEnvironment.org for cleaning products.

RECYCLING AND REUSING. Need we say more? Minimize the waste you send to landfills, where decomposition releases a major share of greenhouse gas emissions. Buy recycled products, which generally take less energy to

make than something brand new, and keep buying products that can be recycled. By now you are familiar with what's expected of us—go to your city's website to learn about its recycling program and get to it.

And look online and around your community for new ways to keep perfectly good stuff in circulation. The Freecycle Network (www.Freecycle.org), a grassroots movement launched in 2003 from Tucson, Arizona, connects you with people in your area to give away or ask for specific items, all for free. Anything goes (as long as it's legal), and since everyone lives close by, you may score the item in the morning and make arrangements to pick it up as early as that same day. The site encourages users to arrange "transactions" in safe public venues or to have others around them if the pickup is at a home.

FOOD. Given the urgency of global warming, many of us are ready for more drastic steps. Michael Pollan, author of *The Omnivore's Dilemma* and *In Defense of Food: An Eater's Manifesto*, advocates growing your own food. You can't get more local than that.

While you're in the backyard, throw kitchen scraps and fallen leaves into a bin and tend to your compost pile. Change your diet by eating less meat or becoming a vegetarian to make a significant dent in meat demand.

How crucial is this? Producing 1 kg of beef puts 220 times as much carbon into the atmosphere as 1 kg of carrots, and more than 40 times that of bread and 13 times that of chicken, says EarthShift (EarthShift.com), an environmental consulting organization.

Eating fewer packaged and processed foods would also help. Packaging accounts for 7 percent of food product energy use, the Earth Policy Institute says, and it is not uncommon for the energy invested in packaging to exceed that in the food it contains. Another 16 percent of energy used in the lifecycle of food is devoted to canning, freezing, and drying.

CHILDREN. Consider the environment, and adoption, when giving thought to the children you may have. "People usually do not think about this, but the biggest impact your marriage has is how many kids you choose to have," says Anja Kollmuss, an associate scientist with the Stockholm Environment Institute, an affiliate of Tufts University. "I know this is a touchy subject with people, but in a world where the average American consumes twenty times more than the average Indian, family size in the United States has a huge effect on the climate."

Kenneth Green, an environmental scientist and resident scholar with the American Enterprise Institute, says not to forget pets. "Having a couple of dogs is like having another child," he says. "You have to heat and cool the house for them, you have to feed them animal protein. You have to wash them, and buy products for them, all of which carries an environmental price tag."

ACTION AND ADVOCACY. No one can solve the problems of the world alone. But one way to heighten your impact is by joining forces with like-minded people (See "It's Not All About Shopping" on page 166). You can start out by trying to adhere to the provisions of the Live Earth Pledge spearheaded by Nobel Peace Prize Laureate and former Vice President Al Gore. Among them:

VOTE for leaders who share your commitment to solving the climate crisis.

FIGHT for a moratorium on the construction of new coal-fired generating facilities.

DEMAND that our country join an international treaty that commits us to cutting global warming pollution by 90 percent by the next generation.

So as you can see, it's hardly enough to change a light bulb. But step by step, we can make big shifts in our habits for the next generation. It is part of what drives couples like Karin and Patrick. "I don't want my child in polyester sheets and things that are going to off-gas," she says. "I don't want him chewing on phalates in toys."

"Here I am bringing a baby into the world, with tender skin and a tender immune system," she says. "I'm so grateful that we'll have a nontoxic, healthy home that we feel is a piece of heaven on earth."

CALLING HOME DEPOT

If you're in the market for a new home, you will find that right next to "drop-dead views," the owners may try to draw your interest with another tempting feature—"what makes it green," as in thermal solar water heating, low V.O.C. paints, and LEED certification (www.ListedGreen.com.)

"The green housing market is expanding," said Ashley Katz, a spokeswoman with the U.S. Green Building Council in Washington, D.C., which certifies green construction. "The house doesn't have to be more expensive than a conventional home, but any premium you pay you're going to recoup in energy and water savings over the life of the home."

Many couples, though, will buy an existing home or return to their old one after the honeymoon. For guidelines on how to green your kitchen, bathroom, and other rooms in your home, go to the U.S. Green Building Council's GreenHomeGuide.

org. The site offers checklists for renovations and retrofitting, as well as directories for products.

Global Green (www. GlobalGreen.org) says green building products and materials should fall into five major categories: those that 1) save energy; 2) conserve water; 3) contribute to a safe indoor environment; 4) protect natural resources by, for example, using salvaged products or materials with recycled content; and 5) reduce the building's negative

impact on the community, such as cisterns that mitigate the effects of storm water runoff.

Many "must-dos" require simple steps you can take care of yourself with a trip to the hardware store, without the need to hire a contractor. For example:

◎ Re-program the thermostat to save energy

◎ Plug air leaks in windows, doors and walls

◎ Switch to Energy Star appliances

◎ Put aerators in your faucets to reduce the water flow without affecting pressure

◎ Check with your utility company to switch to green power. You can find out what's available at the Department of Energy's Energy Efficiency and Renewable Energy website, www.eere.energy.gov/consumer.

And don't forget to check with your city and home insurer for tax credits and insurance premium discounts related to green measures. To find tax breaks, rebates, and other incentives, go to www.GreenHomeGuide.org/

Rain barrels gather water from the gutter downspout.

resources/incentives.html. Lastly, the green checklist goes beyond the walls of the home, the Green Building Council says. When shopping for a new home, for example, also make sure the property is within walking distance to public transportation; is landscaped with drought-resistant plants rather than water-guzzlers, especially lawns; and was not built on environmentally sensitive areas like farmland or wetlands. And to consume less, buy as small a dwelling as you comfortably can.

Awareness of the environment has come a long way, but one of the interesting questions I frequently encountered was how much green are we really ready for? I noticed a certain hesitation on the part of some environmental groups, apparently out of concern that they would come across as too ambitious in what they asked the public to do. The last thing you want, some groups said, is for people to tune out green messages because they seem to require too many lifestyle sacrifices. "Then you become the crazy environmentalist nobody wants to listen to," said Isabelle Silverman, a legal fellow with the Environmental Defense Fund.

But I found that many brides and grooms felt strongly that their wedding was an opportunity to do more, not less—even when they wanted to hew to old traditions. Once they made the connection between the environmental crisis and their own behavior, these couples were eager to do their part. In fact, they felt doing their part enhanced the meaning and the memories of their wedding rather than detracted from it. It made the celebration more personal, more like them.

Increasingly, we may not have much of a choice. Even in Los Angeles, where cars are viewed not just as essential transportation but as a status symbol, thousands of commuters switched to van pooling and mass transportation when gas prices surpassed $4 a gallon in mid-2008. Higher fuel costs continue to have ripple effects in what we consume and how we consume it.

There are, of course, many ideas about the best way to tackle greenhouse gas emissions and global warming. Some point out that what is urgently required is not small individual steps but major policy leaps by the country at a national level, such as reducing our dependence on coal for electricity production. While such initiatives could have a major impact, the political process sometimes moves slowly. I feel such arguments sometimes underestimate the power, and emotional appeal, of grassroots movements. Changing our individual lifestyles creates an ethical base for bigger changes. It adds to our collective sense of responsibility. It helps build political pressure to force major shifts from our elected officials.

So what role can a wedding play? As stories with happy endings, weddings touch a warm sentimental chord inside all of us. At a wedding, the green message may sink in more effectively because it's given in the context of a joyful celebration, not a lecture or an editorial. And with more than 2 million marriages taking place a year, the message can reach an audience in the tens of millions.

Clearly, the word is spreading. By late 2007, a high-profile green wedding had made it to the pages of the New York Times wedding section, with the marriage of Congresswoman Gabrielle Giffords, a Democratic representative from Arizona, and Cmdr. Mark E. Kelly, a NASA astronaut and Navy pilot. The bride, the article said, wore "recycled Vera Wang" (for more on the gown see Chapter 4: The Dress) and insisted that for the celebration, at an Arizona organic produce farm, "anything that wasn't biodegradable had to be reusable."

With same-sex marriages winning a nod in some states, the way is being paved for even more opportunities for couples to join the trend.

I hope this book has shown you that to minimize your celebration's carbon footprint, set an example for guests, and get your married life started on the right vibe, nothing beats a green wedding. Here is how some brides and grooms feel looking back.

◎ *On having a green wedding:* "We want to be part of making the planet better. It felt like we were doing the right thing and we were being true to ourselves."—*Ali Wood, of Brooklyn, New York*

◎ *On making the effort to find green vendors for the venue, the invitations and other wedding elements:* "I very strongly believe that where you put your money is where everybody will start to put their product. I'm proud of the fact that I put my money into things that are green."—*Kelly Nichols, of Danville, California*

◎ *On choosing a venue (Listening Rock Farm in New York) that donated its fee to research on the endangered pearly mussel:* "To have the wedding on a spot where there's actual research going on for a species that's going extinct, that felt very good. A lot of traditional wedding sites seemed like a corporation. It really felt special that the site fee went to something meaningful."
—*Dr. Michael McKnight, of Brooklyn, New York*

◎ *On offsetting guests' travel:* "We felt that it made our wedding even more personal and special for us, and kept us from feeling guilty about causing so much travel."
—*Elizabeth Levy, of Boston*

◎ *On incorporating a mass transit theme to the wedding:* "I definitely feel good about using one of the most important days of our lives to simultaneously celebrate our lives together and make an important statement to a large audience of people who have the power to instigate change."—*Matt Cherry, of Atlanta*

◎ *On combining a green wedding with a pirate-theme:* "By choosing green you're not putting yourself in a box. We were able to reflect who we were and make a statement. Our friends and families said, 'Of course Stephanie and Mark did this. This is who they are.'"
—*Stephanie Hibbert, of San Francisco*

◎ *On achieving green simplicity with a wedding at an organic farm attended by 250 guests:* "So much of who we are is a commitment to public service, my husband through military service and me by serving in Congress. We saw it as an extension of our commitment to our country and the environment. It was the happiest experience I've ever had and a big part of that was having a wedding that felt right."
—*Congresswoman Gabrielle Giffords, of Tucson, Arizona.*

BIODEGRADABLE: products that will break down and decompose into elements found in nature, thus reentering the environment safely rather than damaging it.

BIODIESEL: an alternative fuel for diesel engines made with vegetable oils or animal fat–based oils. It performs like petroleum-based diesel fuel but produces far lower emissions.

BIODYNAMICS: a method of agriculture that goes beyond organic farming by relying on the farm's own self-sustaining abilities. For example, biodynamics minimizes outside inputs of fertilizers, feed, or pesticides. It relies on crop rotation; recycling of its own water and organic material (such as manure from livestock) for fertilizing; and on the sun, the moon, and the planet's positions as guides for when to plant and harvest. For more information, check the Demeter Association (www.Demeter-USA.org), which certifies biodynamic products.

CARBON EMISSIONS: the release of CO_2, one of the major heat-trapping greenhouse gases causing global warming.

CARBON FOOTPRINT: your personal contribution of CO_2 and other greenhouse gases to the atmosphere through activities such as driving and electricity use.

COMPOSTABLE: Paper, food, leaves, and other items that can decompose into organic matter through composting, the art of turning organic waste into soil-conditioning material.

ECO: short for ecological. Designed to be in harmony with the environment.

FAIR TRADE: In general, the international Fair Trade movement works at protecting the environment while ensuring that workers are paid a living wage and smaller producers get a fair price for their products. You may come across different labels. In the United States, certified fair trade products like coffee, chocolate, honey, and flowers carry the "Fair Trade Certified" label, which pays a premium to producers so that they can invest in community development projects like day care centers and scholarship programs. (Fair Trade can also be organic, but it is not always so.) Another logo, "Fair Trade Federation," from the organization of the same name whose member companies subscribe to Fair Trade goals, extends to handicrafts and non-food products. TransFair USA (www.TransfairUSA.org) has more information on labels.

FOSSIL FUELS: ancient buried remains of plants and animals that are transformed into oil, natural gas, and coal. Energy is produced by extracting and burning these fuels, which releases enormous volumes of greenhouse gases into the air.

GLOBAL WARMING: a slow rise in the earth's temperature caused by the release of greenhouse gases that trap the sun's heat near the planet's surface.

GREEN: environmentally friendly products and activities.

GREENHOUSE GASES: gases that trap heat in the atmosphere. The Environmental Protection Agency says the greenhouse gases released by human activities include carbon dioxide (through the burning of fossil fuels, solid waste, trees, and others), methane (through production and transport of fossil fuels, from livestock and agricultural practices and by the decay of organic waste in solid waste landfills), and nitrous oxide (through agricultural and industrial activities).

GREEN WASHING: falsely claiming to be green.

LOCAL: from your immediate region. Defining local can be a thorny endeavor, but many environmentalists say a 1- to 200-mile radius is an appropriate target area for things like water, food, and energy.

NATURAL: a label deemed too vague and meaningless. For meat and poultry, the Department of Agriculture defines it as minimally processed and containing no artificial ingredients or added color. The U.S. Food and Drug Administration has not established a formal definition for the term, but it does not object to the term on food labels provided the product does not contain added color, artificial flavors, or synthetic substances.

ORGANIC: Under the United States Department of Agriculture (USDA) National Organic Program, organic crops are raised without using most conventional pesticides and without petroleum-based or sewage sludge–based fertilizers. Animals are given no antibiotics or growth hormones and must be fed organic feed and given access to the outdoors. Products that are 95 to 100 percent organic get to display the "USDA Organic" seal. Processed products, like soup, made with at least 70 percent organic ingredients can use the label "Made with organic ingredients." Products with fewer than 70 percent organic ingredients can't use the "Organic" label except to identify the specific organic ingredient in the product.

RECLAIMED: salvaged materials that are returned to use, as in wood recovered from a demolition site.

RECYCLABLE: an item that can be used again in either its original form or as part of a new product, as in paper waste that can be turned into a wedding invitation.

RENEWABLE: resources that can't be depleted or exhausted by our consumption. Renewable sources for energy include sun, wind, water, and biomass or plant matter that is transformed into energy. Renewable materials can quickly replenish themselves, such as bamboo grass.

SUSTAINABLE: the result of practices that "sustain" our natural resources rather than deplete or permanently damage them so as to not undermine the ability of future generations to meet their own needs. Reusing, recycling, and powering your home with renewable energy are all sustainable practices.

BOOKS/MAGAZINES/SHOWS

Blessed Unrest: How the Largest Movement in the World Came into Being and Why No One Saw It Coming (Paul Hawken)

Branded!: How the Certification Revolution is Transforming Global Corporations (Michael E. Conroy)

The Omnivore's Dilemma: A Natural History of Four Meals (Michael Pollan)

In Defense of Food: An Eater's Manifesto (Michael Pollan)

Eating Between the Lines: The Supermarket Shopper's Guide to the Truth Behind Food Labels (Kimberly Lord Stewart)

Flower Confidential: The Good, the Bad and the Beautiful (Amy Stewart)

The New Natural House Book: Creating a Healthy, Harmonious and Ecologically Sound Home (David Pearson)

Natural Home Magazine

Verdant Magazine

Planet Green (24-hour eco-lifestyle television network, also at www.PlanetGreen.discovery.com)

Building Green TV (a television series, also at www. BuildingGreenTV .com)

CAMERA AND VIDEO SITES

CameraRenter
888-387-3683
www.CameraRenter.com

Wedding and Event Videographers Association International
www.weva.com

Atmosfair
www.Atmosfair.de

Carbonfund
1320 Fenwick Lane
Suite 206
Silver Spring, MD 20910
240-293-2700
www.Carbonfund.org

ClimateCare
www.ClimateCare.org

Climate Friendly
http://ClimateFriendly.com

Environmental Protection Agency
http://epa.gov/climatechange/emissions/ind_calculator.html

Expedia
www.Expedia.com

Global Footprint Network
www.FootprintCalculator.org

MyClimate
www.MyClimate.org

NativeEnergy
www.NativeEnergy.com

Terrapass
415-692-3411
877-210-9581
www.Terrapass.com

Trx Travel Analytics
440-248-4111
http://carbon.trx.com

Demeter USA (for biodynamic farms and products)
Philomath, OR
541-929-7148
www.Demeter-USA.org

Fair Trade Federation
202-636-3547
www.FairTradeFederation.org

Forest Stewardship Council
11100 Wildlife Center Drive
Suite 100
Reston, VA 20190
703-438-6401
www.fscus.org

Oregon Tilth
470 Lancaster Dr. NE
Salem, OR 97301
503-378-0690
www.Tilth.org

Scientific Certification Systems
510-452-8000
www.scscertified.com

Transfair (for Fair Trade Certified)
1500 Broadway, Suite 400
Oakland, CA 94612
510-663-5260
www.TransfairUSA.org

United States Department of Agriculture (for USDA
Organic)
www.usda.gov

U.S. Green Building Council (for LEED)
1800 Massachusetts Avenue NW
Suite 300
Washington, DC 20036
800-795-1747
www.usgbc.org

Veriflora
www.Veriflora.com

The Alliance for Climate Protection - We Campaign
www.WeCanSolveIt.org

Campaign for Safe Cosmetics
www.SafeCosmetics.org

Cary Institute of Ecosystem Studies
Plant Science Building
2801 Sharon Turnpike
Millbrook, NY 12545
845-677-5343
www.ecostudies.org

Conservatree
415-883-6264
www.Conservatree.org

Consumers Union
www.GreenerChoices.org

Co-op America's "National Green Pages"
www.CoopAmerica.org

Earth Island Institute
300 Broadway, Suite 28
San Francisco, CA 94133
www.EarthIsland.org

Earth Pledge
www.EarthPledge.org

Earth Policy Institute
www.Earth-Policy.org

Earthshift
www.EarthShift.com

Ecological Society of America
1990 M Street, NW, Suite 700
Washington, DC 20036
202-833-8773
www.esa.org

Environmental Defense Fund
257 Park Avenue South
New York, NY 10010
212-505-2100
www.edf.org

Environmental Paper Network
www.EnvironmentalPaper.org

Environmental Working Group
www.ewg.org

The Federal Trade Commission
www.ftc.gov

Global Footprint Network
312 Clay Street, Suite 300
Oakland, CA 94607
510-839-8879
www.FootprintNetwork.com

Global Green USA
www.GlobalGreen.org

Global Witness
1120 19th Street, West, 8th Floor
Washington, DC 20036
202-721-5670
www.GlobalWitness.org

Greenopia
www.Greenopia.com

www.GreenwashingIndex.com

National Geographic Society's "Green Guide"
www.TheGreenGuide.com

Natural Resources Defense Council
212-727-2700
www.nrdc.org

Oxfam International
www.Oxfam.org

Organic Consumers Association
www.OrganicConsumers.org

Organic Trade Association
www.ota.com

Rainforest Alliance
665 Broadway, Suite 500
New York, NY 10012
212-677-1900
www.rainforest-alliance.org

Redefining Progress
1326 14th Street NW
Washington, DC 20005
202-234-9665
www.rprogress.org

Sierra Club
85 Second Street, 2nd Floor
San Francisco, CA 94105
415-977-5500
www.SierraClub.com

Stockholm Environment Institute
www.sei.-us.org

Tufts Climate Initiative
www.tufts.edu/tei

United States Agency for International Development
www.usaid.gov

Women's Voices for the Earth
www.WomenandEnvironment.org

DONATIONS AND PHILANTHROPY

ABC Home & Planet Foundation
www.ABCHomeandPlanet.org

American Diabetes Association
www.diabetes.org

CharityGiftCertificates.org
www.CharityGiftCertificates.org

Doctors Without Borders
333 7th Avenue, 2nd Floor
New York, NY 10001
888-392-0392
212-679-6800
www.DoctorsWithoutBorders.com

Fairy Godmothers
www.FairyGodmothersInc.com

Heifer International
1 World Avenue
Little Rock, AR 72202
800-422-0474
www.heifer.org

I Do Foundation
www.IDoFoundation.org

JustGive
312 Sutter Street
Suite 410
San Francisco, CA 94108
866-587-8448
415-982-5700
www.JustGive.org

Making Memories Breast Cancer Foundation
12708 SE Stephens Street
Portland, OR 97233
503-829-4486
www.MakingMemories.org

Society for the Prevention of Cruelty to Animals
SPCA International
P.O. Box 1230
Washington, DC 20013
www.spca.org

World Wildlife Fund
202-293-4800
www.WorldWildlife.org

DRESS DESIGNERS

David's Bridal
www.DavidsBridal.com

Conscious Clothing
505-982-7506
www.GetConscious.com

Elisa Jimenez
www.ElisaJ.com

Figleaves.com
866-751-2598
www.Figleaves.com

Linda Loudermilk
63 Pearl Street
Brooklyn, NY 11201
718-797-2557
www.LindaLoudermilk.com

PreOwnedWeddingDresses.com
www.PreOwnedWeddingDresses.com

Threadhead Creations
865-288-0391
www.ThreadheadCreations.com

Tuija Asta Järvenpää
www.saumadesign.net/Jarvenpaa.htm

ECOTOURISM

Backroads
800-462-2848
510-527-1555
www.Backroads.com

Copamarina Beach Resort & Spa
Road 333 Km 6.5, Cana Gorda
Guanica, Puerto Rico 00653
800-468-4553
www.Copamarina.com

Earthwatch Institute
www.Earthwatch.org

Environmentally Friendly Hotels
www.EnvironmentallyFriendlyHotels.com

Ethical Traveler
www.EthicalTraveler.org

Green Hotels Association
www.GreenHotels.com

Habitat for Humanity
www.habitat.org

Hands Up Holidays
www.HandsUpHolidays.com

The International Ecotourism Society (TIES)
www.ecotourism.org

Lonely Planet
www.LonelyPlanet.com

Moon Travel Guides
www.Moon.com

The Nature Conservancy
www.Nature.org

Planeta.com
www.Planeta.com

ResponsibleTravel.com
www.ResponsibleTravel.com

Rough Guides
www.RoughGuides.com

Sierra Club Outings
www.SierraClub.org/outings

Sustainable Travel International
www.SustainableTravelInternational.org

United Nations Environment Programme
www.uneptie.org

WorldSurface.com
www.worldsurface.com

Zion National Park
Springdale, UT 84767
435-772-3256
www.nps.gov/zion/

FLOWERS

California Pajarosa Floral
133 Hughes Road
Watsonville, CA 95076
831-722-6374
www.pajarosa.com

EcoFlowers.com
866-518-8070
www.EcoFlowers.com

Organic Bouquet
877-899-2468
www.OrganicBouquet.com

Organic Style
www.OrganicStyle.com

The Spiraled Stem Floral Design
3930 E. Miraloma Avenue, Suite H
Anaheim, CA 92806
714-632-6885
www.TheSpiraledStem.com

FOOD AND DRINK

Alter Eco Fair Trade
2339 Third Street, Suite 15
San Francisco, CA 94107
415-701-1212
www.AlterEco-usa.com

Brick House Vineyards
18200 NE Lewis Rogers Lane
Newberg, OR 97132
503-538-5136
www.BrickHouseWines.com

Butte Creek Brewing
945 West 2nd Street
Chico, CA 95928
530-894-7906
www.ButteCreek.com

Chef Stephanie
415-810-2433
www.Chef-Stephanie.com

Divine Chocolate
www.DivineChocolate.com

Eat Well Guide
212-991-1858
www.EatWellGuide.org

Ecofish
www.Ecofish.com

Environmental Defense Fund Seafood Selector
www.edf.org/documents/1980_pocket_seafood_selector.pdf

Finnegans Irish Amber
www.finnegans.org

Frey Vineyards
14000 Tomki Road
Redwood Valley, CA 95470
707-485-5177
www.FreyWine.com

Green Mountain Coffee Roasters
888-879-4627
www.GreenMountainCoffee.com

Hotlix
800-328-9676
www.hotlix.com

Local Harvest
220 21st Avenue
Santa Cruz, CA 95062
831-475-8150
www.LocalHarvest.org

Monterey Bay Aquarium Seafood Watch
www.SeafoodWatch.org

Numi Organic Tea
www.NumiTea.com

Organic Vintners
1628 Walnut Street
Boulder, CO 80302
303-245-8773
800-216-3898
www.OrganicVintners

Theo Chocolate
www.TheoChocolate.com

Wolaver's Certified Organic Ales
802-388-0727
www.OtterCreekBrewing.com/wolavers.html

World Centric (for disposable tableware)
2121 Staunton Court
Palo Alto, CA 94306
650-283-3797
www.WorldCentric.org

GREEN BUILDING

American Lung Association – Health House
www.HealthHouse.org

Energy Star
www.EnergyStar.gov

Listed Green Homes
www.ListedGreen.com

Living Homes
2910 Lincoln Blvd.
Santa Monica, CA 90405
310-581-8500
www.LivingHomes.net

Olson Homes
www.OlsonHomes.com

United States Green Building Council
www.usgbc.org
www.GreenHomeGuide.org

Bag, Borrow or Steal
www.BagBorroworSteal.com

Branch: Sustainable Design for Living
415-626-1012
www.BranchHome.com

Charmoné Shoes
www.Charmone.com

Craigslist
www.Craigslist.org

Ecco Bella
www.EccoBella.com

Gaiam: A Lifestyle Company
877-989-6321
www.Gaiam.com

Global Exchange
4018 24th Street (near Noe)
San Francisco, CA 94114
415-648-8068
800-805-4410
www.gxonlinestore.org

GreenandMore.com
877-473-3616
www.GreenandMore.com

GreenFeet
888-562-8873
www.GreenFeet.com

The Green Glass Company
5801 Stella Avenue
Weston, WI 54476
715-355-1897
www.GreenGlass.com

GreenSage.com: Sustainable Furnishings & Materials
www.GreenSage.com

I'm Over It
877-834-3516
www.ImOverItOnline.com

MINK Shoes
310-927-4247
www.MinkShoes.com

Moo Shoes
78 Orchard Street
New York, NY 10002
212-254-6512
www.MooShoes.com

Organic Style
877-899-2468
www.organicstyle.com

The Road Less Traveled
2202 ½ North Main Street
Santa Ana, CA 92706
714-836-8727
www.roadlesstraveledstore.com

Té Casan
382 West Broadway
New York, NY 10012
212-584-8000
www.TeCasan.com

Ten Thousand Villages
717-859-8100
www.TenThousandVillages.com

3r Living
276L Fifth Avenue
Brooklyn, NY 11215
718-832-0951
www.3rliving.com

Uncommon Goods
888-365-0056
www.UncommonGoods.com

VivaTerra
800-233-6011
www.VivaTerra.com

www.WeddingChannel.com

World of Good
www.OriginalGood.com
www.WorldofGoodInc.com

INVESTING

Calvert Foundation
800-248-0337
www.CalvertFoundation.org

Community Investing Center
www.CommunityInvest.org

Domini Social Investments
www.domini.com

INVITATIONS

eInvite.com
888-346-8483
www.eInvite.com

InviteSite
450 S. Raymond Avenue
Pasadena, CA 91105
626-793-4600
888-349-4684
www.InviteSite.com

Oblation Papers & Press
www.OblationPapers.com

Of the Earth
888-294-1526
www.custompaper.com

JEWELRY

Apollo Diamond Inc.
www.ApolloDiamond.com

Bling Yourself
www.BlingYourself.com

Brilliant Earth
800-691-0952
www.BrilliantEarth.com

Etsy
www.etsy.com

GreenKarat
877-330-4605
www.GreenKarat.com

Leber Jeweler
303 West Erie Street
Chicago, IL 60610
312-944-2900
www.LeberJeweler.com

No Dirty Gold
202-887-1872
www.NoDirtyGold.org

Sumiche Jewelry
541-896-9841
www.sumiche.com

Back to Earth
1327 61st Street
Emeryville, CA 94608
510-652-2000
www.BacktoEarth.com

Barr Mansion and Artisan Ballroom
10463 Sprinkle Road
Austin, TX 78754
512-926-6907
www.BarrMansion.com

Carver Park Reserve
Lake Auburn Campground
7200 Victoria Drive
Minnetrista, MN 55364
www.ThreeRiversParkDistrict.org

Casa de la Vista – Treasure Island
www.sfgov.org/site/treasureisland_page.asp?id=294

dvGreen
787 Ninth Avenue, Suite 2S
New York, NY 10019
212-713-0013
www.dvGreen.com

Fresh Events Company
1510 Oxley Street, Suite F
South Pasadena, CA 91030
626-755-4362
www.FreshEventsCompany.com

Gale Woods Farm
7210 County Road 110 W.
Minnestrista, MN 55364
763-694-2001
www.ThreeRiversParkDistrict.org

Girari Sustainable Furniture and Furnishings
www.Girari.com

Inn of the Seventh Ray
128 Old Topanga Canyon Road
Topanga, CA 90290
310-455-4311
www.InnoftheSeventhRay.com

Joe Moller Events
310-993-6909
www.JoeMoller.com

Listening Rock Farm
Wassaic, NY
www.ListeningRockFarm.com

Sturtevant Camp
P.O. Box 847
Sierra Madre, CA 91025
760-249-4626
www.SturtevantCamp.org

Treasure Island
415-274-0660
www.sfgov.org/site/treasureisland_index.asp

Vibrant Events
San Francisco, CA
415-839-9665
www.VibrantEvents.net

Wildwood Acres Resort
1055 Hunsaker Canyon
Lafayette, CA 94549
925-283-2600
www.WildwoodAcres.com

Zilker Metropolitan Park
2100 Barton Springs Road
Austin, TX 78746
512-974-6700
www.ci.austin.tx.us/zilker/

WebcastMyWedding.net
229-389-9905
www.WebcastMyWedding.net

Live Vows Wedding Webcasts
PO Box 15561
Panama City, FL 32406
877-968-7182
www.LiveVows.com

www.MyEvent.com

www.MyWedding.com

www.WedShare.com

www.WedQuarters.com

www.WeddingWebsites.com

www.WeddingWindow.com

American Enterprise Institute for Public Policy Research
1150 Seventeenth Street, NW
Washington, DC 20036
202-862-5800
www.aei.org

The Emily Post Institute
www.EmilyPost.com

Etiquette Now!
www.EtiquetteNow.com

EPA Green Vehicle Guide
www.epa.gov/greenvehicles

Freecycle
www.Freecycle.org

Green Festival
www.greenfestivals.org

Live Earth Pledge
www.LifeEarthPledge.org

Minnesota Renewable Energy Society
2928 5th Avenue South
Minneapolis. MN 55408
612-308-4757
www.MNRenewables.org

MyRegistry.com
www.MyRegistry.com

Portovert
www.Portovert.com

TheKnot
www.theKnot.com

TreeHugger
www.TreeHugger.com

U.S. Department of Energy – Energy Efficiency and
Renewable Energy
www.eere.energy.gov

Social Funds
www.SocialFunds.com

Social Investment Forum
www.SocialInvest.org

United States Department of the Treasury's Community
Development Financial Institutions Fund
www.cdfifund.gov/awardees/db/index.asp

ACKNOWLEDGMENTS

My husband, Jim, pointed out this would be the perfect first book after more than two decades of newspaper writing. Jim, my love, thank you for your support and for your work as first-line editor. Your fingerprints (and groom perspective) can be found in many chapters.

I thank my agent, Tamar Rydzinski, for championing *Green Wedding*, and Stewart, Tabori & Chang for greening this book with recycled paper and for investing in a hardcover with beautiful art. Thanks to my editor, Dervla Kelly, for her dedication to the project and for making sure the text was accompanied by pictures showing green weddings in all their gorgeousness, no matter the couple's budget or style. I'm also grateful to my editors at the New York Times for giving me the time to finish the project when the time crunch became overwhelming.

Several author friends offered advice and moral support—Lynn, Dana, Gary: thank you. Apologies to my stepchildren, Marina and Sam, who saw me drop out of their lives on weeknights and weekends while I toiled away. Sorry for missing the jazz drum concerts and family dinners.

Several pioneers in the green market offered invaluable guidance: event planners Corina Beczner of Vibrant Events in San Francisco, Danielle Venokur of dvGreen in New York, and Eric Fenster of Back to Earth in Emeryville, California; flower designer Christine Saunders of The Spiraled Stem in Anaheim, California; and Delilah Snell, owner of The Road Less Traveled in Santa Ana, California. They are as much educators as they are business people.

But mostly I owe thanks to the stars of *Green Wedding*, the fearless couples whose love for the planet is redefining the American wedding. For diving into uncharted waters so that others could follow, I thank:

◎ Margo Kaplan and Benjamin Gibson, of Brooklyn, New York

◎ Kelly Nichols and Alan Puccinelli, of Danville, California

◎ Karin Ascot and Patrick Van Haren, of Austin, Texas

◎ Stephanie Hibbert and Mark Pearson, of San Francisco

◎ Joshua Houdek and Kristi Papenfuss, of Minneapolis

◎ Elizabeth Roberts and Michael McKnight, of Brooklyn, New York

◎ Lesley and Jason Whyard, of Bergen County, New Jersey

◎ Haily Zaki and Brian Tuey, of Los Angeles

◎ Elizabeth Levy and Ryan Bouldin, of Boston

◎ Anna and Matt Cherry, of Atlanta

◎ Katie Malouf and Joe Bous, of Washington, D.C.

◎ Ali Wood and Kevin Meeker, of Brooklyn, New York

◎ Flora Kiggundu and Martin Serugga, of Kampala, Uganda

◎ Jen Belbis and Eric Bassik, of Los Angeles

◎ Gabrielle Giffords and Mark E. Kelly, of Tucson, Arizona

◎ Kay Moonstar and Stephen Platt, of Los Angeles

PHOTO CREDITS

Page 2 and back cover: © Doberenz Photography, www.doberenzphotography.com, (512) 925-4810

Pages 8, 143: © Tyler Schmitt

Pages 10, 14, 27, 44, 46, 60 (left image), 61, 78, 99, 108, 110, 119, 124, 136, 137, 141 (right image), 145 (right image), 146, 172, 176, 180, 197: © Meg Smith

Pages 13, 33, 34, 60 (right image): © Joshua Houdek, photographs by Pat O'Loughlin of Sandhill Photography

Pages 17, 18, 21, 59, 73, 101, 130 (top and bottom left images), 142: © Andrew Van Gundy

Pages 22, 92, 96, 100, 107: © Boutwell Studio, www.boutwellstudios.com, flowers by Spiraled Stem

Pages 24, 104, 130 (top and bottom right images): © Agaton Strom

Pages 26, 30, 38, 39, 62 and back cover, 145 (left image): © Una Knox

Page 28: © Stella Alesi Photography

Page 29: © The Spiraled Stem Floral Design, photography by Kendra Duerst

Pages 35, 36, 68, 76, 117: © Brenda Ladd Photography

Pages 40, 41, 42: © Photographs courtesy of Yael Ben-Zion, www.yaelbenzion.com

Page 43 (top image): © Forever Photography

Pages 43 (bottom image), 133: © Eric Von Lehmden

Pages 49, 102 (left image), 140: © Vito Kwan

Pages 50, 51, 54, 55, 86: © Kelly Nichols Puccinelli

Page 53: © Delilah Snell, Road Less Traveled Store

Page 56 (left image): © MyRegistry.com

Page 56 (right image): © Lauren Bilanko

Page 65: © Greg Huebner

Page 66: © Stephanie Diani

Page 70: © Couture dress: Elisa Jimenez, The Hunger World 2008, photo © Moe Nadel

Page 72: © Dan Snyder

Pages 75, 95, 106: © Henshall Photography

Page 81: © eInvite.com

Page 82: © WeddingWindow.com, Shutterstock

Page 85: © Kevin Graham, photographer for Of the Earth

Page 88: Image provided courtesy of WeddingWebsites.com

Page 90: © WeddingWindow.com

Pages 102 (right image), 113, 114, 127: © Eric Limon, www.maweddingphotographers.com

Page 116: © Ashley Zeltzer

Page 118: © *Native*Energy, Inc.

Page 122: © Kelly Durham, www.thespiritofphotography.com

Pages 128, 134, 135: © Julio Duffoo Photography

Page 132: © Organic Vintners

Page 138: © Back to Earth

Page 139: © Bennett Sell-Kline

Page 141 (left image): © Daniel Lorenze

Page 144: © Robert Scott Thomas

Page 149: © Eric Bassik

Page 150: © James Sterngold

Pages 153, 154: © Hands up Holidays

Page 156: © Artisan Events

Page 157: © Jennifer Belbis

Pages 158, 162, 163: © Benjamin Sklar

Page 161: © William Hare

Page 164: © CJ Berg Photographics/Sunshine Divis Photography

Page 168: © Freecycle.org

Pages 170, 171: © Pamela Geismar

Front cover: © Meg Smith, flowers and design by Kathleen Deery, wedding planner: Kristi Amoroso

Back cover far left: © Meg Smith, bouquet by Ariella Chezar

Back cover left: © Meg Smith

INDEX

ABOUT THE AUTHOR

MIREYA NAVARRO wrote Green Wedding while working as the West Coast Style correspondent for the *New York Times*, covering lifestyle trends and the entertainment community. She later became the newspaper's environmental writer based in New York. Navarro shared in the Pulitzer Prize for national reporting in 2001 for the *New York Times* series "How Race is Lived in America." Visit her website at www.mireyanavarro.com

MONICA ALMEIDA